The CALVIN INSTITUTE OF CHRISTIAN WORSHIP LITURGICAL STUDIES Series, edited by John D. Witvliet, is designed to promote reflection on the history, theology, and practice of Christian worship and to stimulate worship renewal in Christian congregations. Contributions include writings by pastoral worship leaders from a wide range of communities and scholars from a wide range of disciplines. The ultimate goal of these contributions is to nurture worship practices that are spiritually vital and theologically rooted.

Published

The Pastor as Minor Poet
M. Craig Barnes

What Language Shall I Borrow? The Bible and Christian Worship
Ronald P. Byars

Touching the Altar: The Old Testament and Christian Worship
Carol M. Bechtel, Editor

Christian Worship Worldwide: Expanding Horizons, Deepening Practices
Charles E. Farhadian

Gather into One: Praying and Singing Globally
C. Michael Hawn

The Substance of Things Seen: Art, Faith, and the Christian Community
Robin M. Jensen

*Wonderful Words of Life:
Hymns in American Protestant History and Theology*
Richard J. Mouw and Mark A. Noll, Editors

The Pastor as Minor Poet

Texts and Subtexts
in the Ministerial Life

M. Craig Barnes

William B. Eerdmans Publishing Company
Grand Rapids, Michigan

Wm. B. Eerdmans Publishing Co.
Grand Rapids, Michigan
www.eerdmans.com

Library of Congress Cataloging-in-Publication Data

Barnes, M. Craig.
The pastor as minor poet: texts and subtexts
in the ministerial life / M. Craig Barnes.
p.   cm.   — (The calvin institute of christian worship liturgical studies)
Includes bibliographical references.
ISBN 978-0-8028-2962-7 (pbk.: alk. paper)
1. Pastoral theology.   2. Clergy.   3. Pastoral theology — Anecdotes.
4. Clergy — Anecdotes.   I. Title.

BV4014.B27   2009
253 — dc22

2008036170

For my wife, Dawne, the morning light
beside me on the porch

Contents

PART I

The Call of the Minor Poet

CHAPTER 1

Who Is the Pastor?

I was just trying to get to my office at the church. I had taken too long with my sermon preparations at home, and now a full schedule of appointments and an overflowing inbox were impatiently waiting. But I had promised Mary Jefferson that I would stop by the hospital this morning to pray for her husband before his surgery. Now I was running late. "Running late." I thought about the irony of that phrase.

The parking lot at the hospital was jammed full, and by the time I finally found a place to dump the car and hauled my way up to the seventh floor, the orderlies were wheeling Mr. Jefferson out of his room. I asked them to stop for "a quick prayer," which they did without bothering to hide their irritation. As I walked away, it occurred to me that quick prayers are probably also irritating to God.

The drive from the hospital to the church was just long enough for me to think through the day's appointments: a meeting with the associate pastor to talk about the cost overruns on the mission trip to Mexico; a worship planning session with the Director of Music (need to remember to tell her that the anthems are getting too long again); a lunch meeting with the presbytery's Committee on Ministry, and three appointments with parishioners in the afternoon. (I really hope Bob and Carol Stratton are coming to tell me that they're leaving the church. What a relief that would be.) Oh yeah — I have to call Ted Lambert, who is torqued at the custodian about something. It's always something with Ted. I decide to swing back by the hospital to check on Mr. Jefferson before the church dinner in the Fellowship Hall. But if the day jams up with other stuff (of course it will), I'll see him on my way home from the meeting with the Strategic Planning Committee after the dinner.

As I walk through the office door, I remember those strange words from the text I was working on in my home study less than an hour ago: "Enter through the narrow gate . . ."

I'M A PASTOR. I like pastors; I understand them and believe in their high calling. But this is not an easy time for us. My hunch is that it has never been easy, if the job was done well, but the ministry is now difficult for new reasons.

The hardest thing about being a pastor today is not the long hours, the demanding congregations, the eclectic responsibilities, the fishbowl existence, or the relentless returns of Sundays. Those who have taken the vows of ordination have long shouldered all of that as the yoke of Christ. But only within the last two generations have the clergy been forced to bear an additional burden that is far from light — confusion about what it means to be the pastor.

When my students at the seminary talk about this confusion, they're quick to blame our consumer culture. There's certainly credibility to this explanation. Every day the North American pastor encounters parishioners who have discovered no higher aspiration than to be good consumers with a right to get what they want, when they want it, and how they want it. So when they come to church, they assume that the pastor has no calling other than to create satisfied customers, or they can always take their tithe dollars to the place down the street. This has reduced the pastor to a store manager to whom one complains when the service is not satisfactory. Those of us in church leadership who have become skilled at marketing our programs and dynamic worship services are not without blame when congregations reduce us to service providers. They're only asking for the products we peddle. And we peddle them because we want very much to have a more successful enterprise than that place down the street.

Yes, there is all of that, but our identity confusion cannot be blamed merely on consumerism.

Even the various agendas for pastors that on the surface appear spiritual are problematic: when added together they create a very complicated vocational identity. Some want their minister to be an extrovert who loves to hang out in the halls of the church with a gift for the chat. But others want an introvert who is not intimidated by spending long hours in the study preparing profound sermons. Some want us to be at ease around children, others in the nursing home. Some want to hear sermons that are all about the call to social justice; others just want to hear that they are God's beloved. Some want a pastor who knows how to run a church, while others want a pastor who is good at empowering lay leaders (which often means running the church but giving the credit to lay leaders). No one but the pastor is worried about the inherent contradictions of these definitions of ministry.

The professional literature, offering competing identities for ministers, has only exacerbated the contemporary confusion. Some authors assume that we are at heart therapists or specialists in family systems theory. Others write as if we are all religious entrepreneurs who are dying to build a megachurch. Still others think of the pastor as a mystic wannabe who just needs to check into a monastery to be a monk for a day. Much of the current literature on leadership that is being taught in our seminaries has come from secular universities such as the Harvard Business School. It's presented as if the principles of corporate management can easily be baptized for leaders of congregations.

Denominational leaders, bishops, and those in authority over pastors routinely require them to attend sexual harassment workshops, which have been constructed with the assumption that parish clergy are at their core a scandal waiting to happen — the legacy of that has been to make pastors afraid of both their congregations and themselves.

Confronted with all of these competing identities, is it any wonder that the pastor has been reduced to what Stanley Hauerwas calls "a quivering mass of availability"?[1] Clearly this is not what the Holy Spirit had in mind on the day the pastor was ordained.

Reflective pastors will often attempt to defend against all of these projected identities by looking deep into their hearts and asking, "Who do I think I am?" But our hearts are also conflicted. Even if we succeed in withdrawing into our hearts, it usually feels like a bad committee meeting is going on in there — so many internalized voices are vying for attention and trying to hijack the agenda. Pastors still hear the anxieties of their parents

---

1. Quoted in William Willimon, *Pastor: The Theology and Practice of Ordained Ministry* (Nashville: Abingdon Press, 2002), p. 60.

and in-laws, who wondered out loud if anyone earned a good income in the ministry, the conversations with recently visited friends from college who went to law school and now live in enormous homes, and the stinging criticism from an anonymously written letter signed "In Christ."

Worst of all, pastors keep returning to their own debates about whether or not they were ever told by God to do this job that feels impossible. "Did I just imagine that I was called? Do I really even belong in the ministry? And is it too late to start over at something else? I've always liked woodworking. . . ."

Few pastors will deny that on Sunday mornings we look across the pulpit into the pews with a sense of envy. Everyone else in the church came because they wanted to be there. They're all free. They don't have to praise God even when they feel like cursing today. They could have just spent the morning with *The New York Times* and a good cup of Starbuck's without anyone thinking that their call was in jeopardy. Parishioners are freed by a spiritual anonymity pastors will never know. Best of all, they're free to tell the old ladies with thin lips that they can take a flying leap if they complain one more time. Pastors have none of these freedoms, and they resent that so much of their individuality was lost on the day of their ordinations. But if you asked most pastors to identify this lost individuality, they would have a hard time finding it, because they've assimilated too many projected ones. Carrying so great a burden, it's no wonder they cannot fit through the narrow gate into the Kingdom of God, where all of the freedom of Christ is enjoyed.

The Myth of the Constructed Identity

It should not be surprising that the clergy are struggling with identity issues, since nearly everyone else is as well these days. That's because we now assume that identity is something we construct for ourselves.

Such a strange idea would never have occurred to previous generations, who accepted identity as an inheritance from the family that told their children who they were and, thus, what they would do. It didn't really matter if their kids wanted to be a cobbler, a mother, a serf, or even a king. If that's what their parent did, it was their lot in life as well. And they did that work because it was an expression of who they were. Doing always flowed out of being. Somehow we managed to turn that around about fifty years ago.[2] Now we assume that our identity, being, is determined by what we do. And what we do is totally up to us to decide for ourselves.

When my siblings and I were children, our favorite uncle would put us on his knee and ask, "And what do you want to be someday?" The expected answer would involve something that a person does. No child was expected to say, "I want to be happy." The assumption behind the uncle's question is that we can be anything we want to be, and the way we determine what we will be is primarily through a vocational choice, something we'll do.

From the time we got off that uncle's knee, we were bombarded with more choices than any generation has ever faced in life. If our parents were caring, they took these choices seriously, and used them as a way of helping us discern between good and bad ones. Decisions about Little League, dance, friends, camps, television, smoking, drinking, and whether we wanted to go to church or not eventually matured into choices about college. That's when the self-construction of life began in earnest. So no longer does a family spend the formative years of a child's life inculcating a particular identity, which is the inalienable right of that child to maintain regardless of what the future holds. Now the agenda is to raise children to become proficient at making good choices so that when they leave home they can begin the process of assembling a good future for themselves. Somehow.

During the college years we discovered that if we did not find our choices to be fulfilling, then we could simply choose again and change our majors or even transfer to a different school that would prepare us for a different life. It was easy. We just had to walk over to the registrar's office, fill out a form, and suddenly we were on our way to becoming a successful lawyer instead of a doctor. After our schooling was completed, we maintained this notion of being free to respond to the lack of fulfillment by choosing again. And the assumption was that it should still be easy. If the job was not satisfying, we had a right to get another one, and someone ought to hire us.

It isn't the rearranging of work that is new but the assumption that you can find a job that fulfills your being that is more revolutionary than we realize. I once asked my grandmother if my granddad was fulfilled as a

---

2. For a thesis on how this transformation occurred, see my previous book, *Searching for Home: Spirituality for Restless Souls* (Grand Rapids: Brazos Press, 2003), pp. 37-69.

farmer. She was confused by the question. First I had to explain the concept to her. Finally she shrugged and said, "I don't know, honey. He was a farmer." That was the first time it hit me that he spent most of his life plowing dirt but never asking himself if this was what he wanted to do with his life. He farmed because he inherited the identity of farmer from the six generations of ancestors who lived on that same acreage. That now seems, well, quaint. We understand the pursuit of fulfillment all too well — it's pretty much our Holy Grail.

This search for an identity with which we are content is not limited to work, but it is most obvious in this pursuit. We also spend an enormous amount of time rearranging life with choices about relationships, children, communities, churches, houses, and other possessions, thinking that we will eventually construct an identity we find fulfilling. As a pastor, I have watched too many of my parishioners use up most of their fleeting years making choices that really don't matter. That's because our ancestors had it right. You cannot determine who you are by what you do. But few people believe that anymore. Why else do we introduce ourselves at parties by telling people how we make a living? We do that because we assume we can make our own lives by the way we construct them for ourselves.

At commencement ceremonies over the last few decades, we told our graduates to dream their own dreams, do their own thing, work hard, and they could be whatever they wanted to be. What we did not tell them was how they could know who it is that they want to be. We might as well have told the graduates, "Sorry, we have nothing for you. You're on your own."

When we stopped burdening our youth with any claims from tradition, not to mention a sacred one, we assumed that individuals just inherently and independently know how to put life together for themselves. But by removing them from the claims of previous generations and religious traditions, we only made it impossible for them to have a means of discerning this basic identity issue. All that is left today is to borrow compelling, popular images of life that have been well-marketed.

The biblical depiction of life begins with the words "In the beginning God . . ." And it ends with a magnificent future that is also created by God. Just about everything in between also testifies to the eternal truth that life is made, redeemed, and certainly blessed by God. It's a gift to be received with humility and gratitude, not an achievement. Most of the biblical narrative for our lives can be seen as the unfolding drama of what happens when we do and do not accept our created identity as males and females made in the image of God, for communion with this Creator.

As our theologians remind us, creation occurred "ex nihilo," or out of nothingness. This means that all things, even the dust with which humanity was created, derive their existence from God. So when we seek a different identity derived from anything other than God, we don't actually become different but only return to the nothingness we were before God created our lives. This is what gathers in the pews of church every Sunday — creatures who believed the serpent's lie that their identity could be changed by reaching for something other than what they were given by the Creator. Some believed they could get a different, preferred identity if they only got married. Others thought they just needed to find a better job or buy a better home in order to have a better life. Still others cling not to dreams but to the hurts of yesterday — as if they could improve the past by holding it so tightly. And all that the reach for a different source to their identity has left them with is souls filled with the primordial nothingness. Having grown exhausted reaching for a preferred self, many just give up and settle for busy or comfortable distractions that numb the emptiness of their souls.

The Christian hope claims that God would not settle so easily. In Jesus Christ, God became flesh to restore being into our nonbeing by reconciling us to the one "in whom we live, and breathe, and have our being." When the Word that was with God, the Word that was God, became flesh and dwelt among us, being was restored into the nothingness we made of our lives and the world (John 1:1-18). As the Holy Spirit binds us to this Word, allowing us to live "in Christ," we recover the life we were created to enjoy ((Eph. 1:3-14). So, to be clear, we don't *make* a living. We *receive* it through our participation in the Christ, who has brought us home to communion with the Creator.

It is hard enough to discern what it means to receive this gracious gift of life in Christ, and then know what we are to do. That is why people need pastors, and it is what the focus of our ministries should be. However, today most pastors cannot even get to this biblical calling without first wading through the pervasive assumptions of the self-created identity.

Not only does this relatively new pursuit defy the biblical notion that life is a created gift, but it also falsely assumes that the self is independent in making this self-construction. The truth is that if God is not creating our lives, then those around us are. The mother now takes fulfillment in

9

her work only if her children grow up as well as she dreams they will. Office workers and teachers expect the affirmation of good reviews from their supervisors and the rewards of promotions and increased remuneration. Lawyers and doctors need their practices to expand. Entrepreneurs consider themselves a success only if the deals go through. Politicians are completely dependent on the affirmation of the public. There is no such thing as a self-constructed life. There is only being in Christ, or there is the nothingness that others create for us.

The clergy struggle with this as much as anyone.

The "Successful" Pastor

It took me a while to figure this out, but most of the pastors who participate in the Doctor of Ministry programs of our seminary are not primarily motivated by a love of scholarship. Most are looking to be understood. I have always been struck by the almost immediate camaraderie that develops among the students in every seminar I teach, simply because they are surrounded by others who understand their unique temptation to nothingness as pastors. Their fatigue and discouragement just pour out onto the seminar table. They also talk about their joys and the new ideas that seem to be working, and certainly talk about the theology that's listed on the syllabus. But the thing that binds them together is the truth that emerges when they start passing around the hard stuff.

"I don't understand what you mean when you say that the church is the mission of Christ," Jeff said while his hand was still raised. I noticed that he had been fidgeting in his chair while I was interpreting a diagram on the chalkboard. Clearly, he couldn't stand it any longer. "I mean, it sounds right. I remember them telling me this stuff in seminary, but it just isn't what the church really is. Not really. I came to my parish three years ago because they said they wanted someone who could shake them out of their complacency, make the church attractive to young adults, and get them back to growing again. But they have sabotaged every effort I've made to do exactly that. Now they're about to spend over a million dollars to repair a pipe organ. Can you believe that? Do you know what I could do with a million bucks for that church? They aren't the least bit interested in the mission of Christ. All the church wants is for me to keep lulling them to sleep."

I sigh, put the chalk down, and tell myself, "Well, here we go again." It's a familiar story, and I know how much this hurts.

In order to enter the D. Min. program, the pastors need to have been serving a church for at least five years, but most have longer tenures. All of them have been at it long enough to collect wounds, and many have not healed well. Some of the wounds came from the congregation. Some were self-inflicted. For too long many have been dancing on the borders of total burnout, trying to fulfill the contradictory expectations of the congregation and their own expectations about success. None of them wants to be remembered as the pastor who was there when the church closed its doors. So they are compelled to succeed, which means they have to do something to keep people coming in those doors. But here's the rub: Whenever they succeed in meeting the expectations of either the older parishioners or the desired visitors, pastors feel deep in their souls that they are simply con artists. They hate having to be whatever is necessary to keep the old guard reassured and the seekers enticed. They learn to be strong but sensitive, profound but playful, prophetic but consensus-building, always available with an open door but always in touch with the sacred — whatever is necessary to engender approval, no matter how inherently inconsistent, all for the elusive prize of being liked.

It wasn't always like this. The old models of leadership may have been patriarchal and domineering. But the new model that states "I'm just here to give you what you want" can hardly still be called leadership, and my students know it. That was at the heart of Jeff's protest. In his wonderful book *Open Secrets*, Richard Lischer describes the many surprises he encountered when he rolled into his first rural parish assignment as a young pastor desperate to succeed. One of the things that startled him the most was the relationship that the congregation had with their former pastor, who was from a different era. He writes, "Everyone respected him, but if someone were to ask 'Did you like Pastor Martin?' they would say 'Like?' then look quizzically at each other and reframe the question."[3] By contrast, contemporary pastors are tempted to measure their success, not to mention fulfillment, precisely by how well-liked they are. That is because even the clergy function in a society that defines individuals and certainly leaders by their ability to fulfill expectations.

---

3. Richard Lischer, *Open Secrets: A Memoir of Faith and Discovery* (New York: Broadway Books, 2001), p. 67.

I have a sign over my door at the seminary that simply says, "It's just church." I'm trying not to make a cynical statement but to offer an invitation to freedom. A pastor's ability to enjoy church is directly related to knowing its limits. The church is not Jesus. It may be the Body of Christ, but only sort of. The Reformers always maintained an important distinction between the visible body, which is weak, and the invisible Body of Christ, which transcends the limitations of the church we see. This frees the pastor not to take the church more seriously than God does. In Christ, God is dying to love the church, quite literally, and is determined to use it in the completion of Christ's mission on earth. But clearly God doesn't expect the church to build the New Kingdom on earth. That will always be accomplished by the ongoing work of the now-ascended Christ completing his work through the Holy Spirit. Similarly, the Triune God maintains the responsibility of completing the divine mission in each person's life, including the pastor's.

So when pastors are trying to evaluate the success of their life's work, they dare not allow the limited and weak body known as church to be their measure. For that, they can only turn back to the Christ they have "put on" in their baptisms. When they do that, preferably every day through the spiritual disciplines, they are renewed in the identity of being not only liked, but God's beloved. This is what actually frees pastors to return to the congregations that have enough problems to assure us that we'll never run out of work. It even allows us to love the church, as Christ does. But our ability to love is tied to our freedom of not needing the church.

Many of my D. Min. students expect me to offer new ideas and strategies for ministry that would make them successful as pastors. There is no shortage of formulas for creating a successfully constructed pastorate being peddled in the professional religious market today. All of these formulas are based on the assumption that pastors need to meet the expectations of those who are already in the church and especially of those who are not there yet. That only contributes to the internal tension that is tearing apart the souls of reflective pastors, who remember holier purposes to the calling to ministry. Sure, they want to be successful. But it doesn't matter how many new worship services they start, or how many seekers they attract, or how praised they are by either the old guard or the new members, their souls will never settle for success at the cost of their souls.

So in class we spend a lot of time forging our way back to clarity on who we are and whose we are. No one can possibly know what to do without this tether, least of all pastors who daily confront a legion of alternative and very tempting identities from which to work. But when we begin with our own identity in Christ and the pastoral call to assist others in becoming fully alive in him, we are freed from the drudgery of being managers and service providers to pursue something much more creative — being poets of the soul.

A good poet is hard to find, and nothing is more tragic than wasting one in a busy office.

CHAPTER 2

The Parish Poet

When Bob and Carol Stratton arrived at my study for their appointment, all of the air in the room immediately disappeared. It was clear that this was going to be a hard hour. Before he even sat down, Bob began his now-familiar litany of complaints about the choir director, and Carol was already fishing around in her purse for a Kleenex. (Why are you already crying? What does that mean?)

"I just don't understand why you keep that woman here," Bob said as he finally settled back into his chair. "She has absolutely no regard for the wonderful heritage of worship in this church, and she insists on driving people away. I've heard from members of your choir, and they're so unhappy that I'd be surprised if there even is a choir in another month. You've got to do something, and do it now."

I was already rubbing my temples as I asked, "What do you want me to do, Bob?"

"Well, I think we all know what needs to be done. What we don't know is if our pastor is a strong enough leader to do it."

"Ah, yes, I understand, but I don't think your concerns are really about me," I responded. (I'm not biting on that.) "Let's get back to the issue that brought you here. What exactly is it about our music that has you so upset?"

After blowing her nose, Carol joined in. "She never uses the anthems our previous director of music, Dr. Adams, wrote. You know he was here for over twenty-five years, and in those days our church was highly regarded in this community. People came just to hear him play the organ. [Is that true? Should it be?] Now it's an embarrassment when that woman gets up there and starts waving her arms in front of the choir."

"So you don't like the way she conducts the choir?" I asked.

"No, it isn't just that." Bob said quickly. "She plays the organ too loudly, she's thrown out all of the music Dr. Adams wrote, and it seems to us that she's just up there performing. Frankly, the music just isn't as good as it should be. You know, pastor, we're a sophisticated congregation [That can't be good], and we're not going to be able to worship with all of this noise she produces."

I sat forward in my chair and as quietly as possible said, "I've noticed that both of you mentioned Ted Adams. He was clearly a great musician, and I know he was also a very close friend of yours. You must miss him a great deal."

They both looked down at the floor, silent, for a very long time.

EVERY PASTOR KNOWS this conversation all too well. Seldom do people make an appointment just to tell us that they're overwhelmed with gratitude. If there isn't a problem in their personal life, then it's usually a problem they have with the church that has brought them to the pastor's study. It has taken me too long to figure this out, but most of the time, even when they're talking about a complaint with the church, the true issue is closer to home.

Complaining is usually a veiled lament about deeper issues of the soul. Since people are unaccustomed to exploring the mystery of their own souls, they will often work out their spiritual anxieties by attempting to rearrange something external, like a church's music program. But it doesn't matter how many changes they make to the environment around them. They will never succeed in finding peace for the angst of the soul until they attend directly to it. This is why people have pastors.

To be of service to the Holy Spirit, who is at work in human lives, the pastor can never reduce ministry to servicing parishioners' complaints about the church. As illustrated in my conversation with the Strattons, that would have resulted in my trying to prove that I was a strong leader by firing the staff member upon whom they had transferred their anger over the loss of a friend. Even if I had been insecure in my identity and allowed them to tell me what I had to do to be a leader, it would have done nothing to contribute to the Strattons' need to grieve the loss of their friend, who left them. That would have resulted only in furthering both their and my illusions of control, and nothing remotely redemptive would have come of it.

I am often unsure that redemption occurs in parishioners' lives even when I do direct them to the true issue. I would have loved to hear Bob or Carol say to me, "I just can't believe Ted Adams left us." But that was more truth than they were prepared to confess at the time. What was clear to me, though, was that unless I invited them to look beneath their complaint to their personal loss, I would only have been part of the distraction that was keeping them from ever finding healing for their hurt.

The only way a pastor can function with the integrity necessary to do this deeper work well is to remain clear about his or her identity in the church.

Help from the Poets

The Bible is filled with enduring, healthy images of pastoral ministry. Some of us are attracted to the image of the shepherd who has sacrificed alternative plans for life and is now willing to lay life down for the sake of the sheep. Others are drawn to the notion of the pastor as priest who stands between God and the people. Still others are attracted to the New Testament notion of the pastor being the witness of the redemptive activity of the ascended and reigning Christ. Some prefer to think of themselves as fulfilling Christ's call to be prophet, priest, and king, but only to the degree that they themselves live in Christ, who alone fulfills his holy offices. And of course, the calling to be ministers of Word and Sacrament can center any pastor. All of these depictions of pastoral identity are more helpful than anything that either congregations or pastors are going to develop without the aid of biblical insights.

I want to suggest still another image: the poet. I present this not as the normative or even preferred image, but simply as another biblical description of the calling of those who have been blessed with a vision that allows them to explore, and express, the truth behind the reality. Poets see the despair and heartache as well as the beauty and miracle that lie just beneath the thin veneer of the ordinary, and they describe this in ways that are recognized not only in the mind, but more profoundly in the soul.

In a day in which people are so profoundly confused about fundamental identity issues, and are desperately trying to construct life as best they can, it is critically necessary for pastors to recover this poetic dimension of their ministries. What the congregation needs is not a strategist to help them form another plan for achieving a desired image of life, but a poet who looks beneath even the desperation to recover the mystery of what it means to be made in God's image.

I believe that all who are called by the Holy Spirit to serve the church as pastors have this poetic vision. It's a necessary ingredient in the mix God uses in creating pastors. Some have cultivated the gift more than others, but all pastors have it, and it's actually impossible to be a pastor without being a poet devoted to making sense of the work of God in human lives. This does not mean that the pastor should end a meeting of the board of trustees by whipping out a few lyrical lines that try to make eternal sense of the budget. Nor does it mean that the pastor torments the congregation with sermons that rhyme. It certainly doesn't mean that pastoral ministry is best understood as a subset of that larger discipline of the humanities called poetry. My interest in the term *poet* is analogical.

Substantive explanations of the ecclesiastical office of the minister are best found in the biblical and theological traditions of the church. There is no shortage of thoughtful, systematic theologies that depict who pastors are called to be and what they are called to do by God. Every denominational tradition develops these. Typically, the early leaders of the various traditions provide the foundational explanations of pastoral ministry. Contemporary theologians then interpret the implications of their theological tradition for the new context in which the ministry occurs today. I'm not challenging any of that. Theology is "first order" reflection, and it is necessary for every pastor to go to school, literally, on this substantive theology. But to gain a fresh perspective on the nature of the person and work of those who sit in the ecclesiastical office, or study, it is helpful to come at the biblical tradition "slant," which is the nature of poets.[1] This is "second order" thinking about the pastor, but that does not make it less critical. When an exhausted pastor is entertaining serious thoughts about applying to law school, it's usually not because the theology failed. Often it's because somewhere along the way it became impossible to make sense of that theology in the midst of the ordinary and relentless messiness of congregational life.

---

1. This borrows from a poem by Emily Dickinson, "Tell all the truth, but tell it slant," in *The Complete Poems of Emily Dickinson* (Boston: Little, Brown, 1960), p. 506.

When I left seminary, I expected my new parishioners would be sitting in the pews with their souls in torment over the existential issues of life, but they were actually sitting there wondering why their teenagers wouldn't talk to them, if it was time to freshen up their resumes, or if they could afford a new boat this year. I thought my committee meetings would be communities of brothers and sisters in Christ who wanted only to lead a mission-oriented church, but more often I encountered bureaucratically oriented volunteers who were in a lather over small things. Like every new pastor, I soon hit upon the dismaying discovery that this congregation wasn't just dying to hear what Karl Barth had to say to them. That didn't mean Barth was irrelevant. It meant only that his first-order writing had to be not simply translated but carried to a realm beneath the presenting issues.

That is how I learned to think poetically about my work and myself. It allowed me to dig beneath all of the talk about budgets, personnel, the recruiting of Sunday school teachers, and who was mad at whom, as well as the more personal concerns about relationships and work, in order to enter the deeper realm where theology makes sense. Only then could I speak to the soul of the congregation about the real choices that make an eternity of difference. To my delight, I discovered that most people eventually become eager to listen with their souls, even if it takes some practice before they are accustomed to it. Like the appreciation of any art, the appreciation of poetry has to be learned. But that's hardly surprising in a society that has successfully inculcated the mythology that anyone's existential crisis really can be resolved with a new boat.

Poets are devoted more to truth than to reality; they are not unaware of reality, but they never accept it at face value. The value of reality is only found by peeling back its appearance to discover the underlying truth. This is why poets care about the text, what is said or done, but only in order to reveal subtext, which reveals what it means. They value the reality they see primarily as a portal that invites them into a more mysterious encounter with truth. This is what distinguishes poets from those whose contributions to society are focused simply on following a particular text. Engineers, for example, follow their textbooks in constructing a bridge that leads across the deep ravines. And one hopes that they have been very, very devoted to those texts. By contrast, a poet who crosses the engineer's bridge will go home and spend all day constructing verse that reveals the longing of the soul to find such an overpass when we stand on the banks of a disaster and peer down into the valley of death.

The last thing anyone sitting in a church pew needs is for the preacher to give advice on following the necessary algorithms for engineering better bridges. Or lessons in economics, politics, or raising children. This doesn't mean that any of these topics are out of bounds for the pastor-poet. But to be faithful to our particular calling, we need to get beneath the reality of what is being said and done to explore the often-mysterious truth of what this means. In making interpretations of this mystery, the pastor is not a free agent but a faithful devotee to his or her biblical and theological tradition of interpretation. This tradition is filled with poetic insights that guide the contemporary pastor into a particular way of uncovering reality to expose the eternal truth. Both the realist and the truth-teller are necessary, but they are seldom found in the same office of leadership.

For example, the civil rights legislation of the 1960s was largely led by President Lyndon Johnson, who often battled a hesitant Congress to secure the passage of more just laws. He was a political realist, and he did what it took to get the votes he needed. Whatever one may think of President Johnson or the other policies of his administration, clearly history has already awarded him with the tribute of being a leader through this significant legislation. But it fell to someone else, a poet, to inspire the nation to accept the dream of a color-blind society. Without the dream, the legislation would never have passed. The Reverend Dr. Martin Luther King Jr. led the country into that dream only by taking us into a painful discovery of the injustice that lurked in the corners of our hearts. That was the truth beneath the reality. But the white majority culture didn't accept this dream easily. The African-American community, whom Dr. King had empowered with one biblical image of freedom after another, led the rest of us to it. They began by marching in the streets, and after the nation watched them mercilessly attacked by police dogs, fire hoses, and angry mobs, they marched into our hearts. But it took a realist and a truth-teller, a politician and a poet.

Pastors are not the only ones working on the Kingdom of God. But they don't help by abandoning their specific call to be poets and taking on the work of the realists and the engineers. Someone has to teach people how to dream.

The Biblical Tradition of Poetry

This is new language to describe the art of pastoral ministry, but it's not a new concept. It's as old as the Old Testament. The biblical poets have expressed the fundamental struggle of all human life, which is alienation from God and the desperate need for redemption. Walter Brueggemann, a professor of Old Testament studies, has demonstrated how the prophets took on the role of national poets who carried on both sides of a sacred conversation between the alienated people and the God who yearns for them.[2] The psalmists also write in such a way as to express both the human and the divine lament within the same breath. This tradition of speaking poetically is carried into the New Testament as well. The Apostle Paul, not typically thought of as a poet, provides the most hopeful stanzas of the Gospel sonnet in presenting Christ as the restoration of our alienated communion with God: "In him we have redemption through his blood, the forgiveness of our trespasses, according to the riches of his grace that he lavished on us" (Eph. 1:7-8). None of these biblical authors accept the realists' explanations that life would be better if only we had a tower that reached to heaven, kings like the other nations, wealth, fewer laws, and a religion that didn't call for so much sacrifice. All of them dig beneath our addiction to the things that keep us from receiving "the riches of his grace."

The church's historic theological poets have drawn from this fundamental biblical drama by providing confessional insights about our lives with and without God. None have done it better than St. Augustine: "Thou hast made us for Thyself, and our hearts are restless till they rest in Thee."[3] There is a reason why this is Augustine's most famous sentence: there has never been a generation for which it is not descriptive of the human heart. This, then, is the function of first-order theological thinking that interprets and expounds upon the meaning of the biblical poetry. The best theologians have done this with a focus more on the eternal truth than on the symptomatic realities that express this truth. So they do not explain not how we find success in the workplace, but explore the restless heart that cannot find its peace.

In contrast to the biblical and theological poets, the pastoral poet has

---

2. Walter Brueggemann, *Finally Comes the Poet: Daring Speech for Proclamation* (Minneapolis: Fortress Press, 1989), p. 49.

3. St. Augustine, Bishop of Hippo, *Confessions: Books I-XIII*, trans. F. J. Shedd (Indianapolis: Hackett Publishing Co., 1993), p. 3.

the unique calling of making sense of their words in light of the dust and grit of daily life in a parish. And unlike those whom society has traditionally revered as poets, whose vision of the deeper reality is nurtured through quiet sanctuary, if not isolation, the pastor-poet lives with a crowded and noisy soul. Central to what it means to be ordained is to open the doors of one's soul to the complexities, pathos, longings, and even sins of those the pastor has vowed to serve.

At the same time, the pastor is even more attentive to the unapparent presence of God among the people of the congregation. One of the reasons that people need pastors is precisely because God is always present but usually not apparent. It takes a poet to find that presence beneath the layers of strategy for coping with the feeling of its absence. Thus, the parish minister's soul becomes a crucible in which sacred visions are ground together with the common and at times profane experiences of human life. Out of this sacred mix, pastors find their deep poetry, not only for the pulpit, but also for making eternal sense out of the ordinary routines of the congregation.

The pastor's days are filled with committee meetings that never end and accomplish little; confirmation classes with kids who can't be cool unless they look bored; races across town to make a hospital call, only to discover that the patient was just discharged *(You're not getting credit for this one)*; counseling sessions with people who don't like their jobs but can't afford to quit them because they need them to afford lifestyles they don't really like either; funerals where we fight back our tears long enough to lead worship; weddings where we fight back the aggressive photographer; conflicts with people who just won't leave the church; and the relentless return of Sundays that demand another profound sermon. And through it all, the attentive pastor is constantly spinning the poetry, helping the congregation to see the sacred subtext of their lives.

As poets, pastors are always looking for a portal that invites passage into a deeper, more mysterious — and thus true — understanding of what is seen. They do this not only in their study of sacred texts but also in their study of the common events of the culture in which we live and in their pastoral conversations, always looking for the mystery that lies just below the surface: *What does it really mean to be "running late"? Is "orderly" an ironic title for someone who pushes you around? The Strattons couldn't possibly be that angry about music.* These parenthetical observations of the poet provide the narrow gate into the truth of our lives.

22

This means that the pastor-poet does his or her best work not with presenting issues, which are seldom the real issue. This is the fallacy of those who try to define the pastor as a manager, an entrepreneur, or a service provider who is only in need of more skills to be a success in handling the many issues that have presented themselves. Most presenting issues are merely symptomatic of underlying theological issues. Even those who treat the pastor as a spiritual leader often reduce his or her work to treating symptoms. Seldom does a day go by without another advertisement appearing in my mail that offers a new product "guaranteed" to make our congregation better at giving, Bible study, and prayer. But if people are not praying, it's the pastor-poet's job to discern why they are hesitant to enter God's presence. And if they are praying, then the question is, Do they really understand what is happening in such sacred communion?

For example, the woman who recently stopped at the door following worship to shake my hand asked me to pray for her in the coming week. "They're deciding if I'm going to make partner in the law firm," she explained. "I've worked really hard for this, so please pray that I get it." My real job at this point is to know that this promotion means too much to her, that she is never going to be satisfied even if she does make partner, that the real source of her identity is her life in Christ, and that if she only prayed to see the sufficiency of this, then she could approach this vote about her status at work with much less anxiety. It is even possible that not making partner will be better for her restless heart than getting what she so desperately wants. But I didn't say any of this. The line is long at the door following worship, and there's no time for all of that. So I say again, "Sure, I'll be praying for you." If I were faithful to my calling, though, the next day I would set up an appointment to have a conversation with her about what is really going on *within* her.

The same thing is true about the legion of church conflicts that are a part of every pastor's life. No amount of good conflict-management skill is going to make us faithful to our real calling. The father of a seventeen-year-old daughter who comes to see me to say he's furious with the youth director for taking the teenagers to the Dominican Republic because "it just isn't safe" is not going to be satisfied even if the trip is moved to Shangri-la. That's because his real worry is that he's about to lose his baby, who's growing up and will soon leave home and his watchful control over her. It doesn't matter if the youth group meets in his basement every week;

she's still going to leave him. It's a necessary loss, part of the created order, and I at least need to know that.

Similarly, when the church board becomes anxious about the budget that's in the red, the pastor cannot react anxiously by taking on the role of a fund-raiser who fixes the problem. What is called for are the strange poetic statements to the congregation that it needs to give its money not because the church has needs, but because we need to be givers. "Fool, this night thy soul shall be required of thee; then whose shall those things be, which you have provided?" (Luke 12:20, KJV).

The Pastor as Minor Poet

T. S. Eliot has claimed that every culture needs minor as well as major poets.[4] The major poets, who are few and far between, provide enduring expressions of the deep truth of life. Minor poets have the more modest goal of inculcating that truth to particular people in particular places.

One of the ways that Eliot distinguishes the major poets is to claim that it is necessary to read the whole body of their work in order to understand any part of it.[5] As time progressed for them, the major poets became focused on an overarching theme that makes sense of everything else they write. It is even possible to claim that eventually the poet became the servant of the poetry and realized that his or her life was devoted to the development of what it was that had to be said. For example, Dante began his career by writing love sonnets in *Vita Nuova,* then studied Scholastic philosophy and published a book of poems on wisdom called *Convivio,* but he ended his life writing the great *Divine Comedy,* which uses Scholastic categories to describe the redemption of the heart's unfaithful love of God. Even his own lack of devotion to the love of his life, Beatrice, became a metaphor for describing the flaw of all human devotion to God. For the last seven centuries we have continued to learn from his enduring classic sonnets that describe the soul's long and at times frightening journey home to God. That's major poetry.

Pastors consider the biblical authors to be their major poets. What

---

4. T. S. Eliot, "What Is Minor Poetry?" in *On Poetry and Poets* (New York: Farrar, Straus & Cudahy, 1957), p. 40.

5. Eliot, "What Is Minor Poetry?" p. 47.

preacher will ever run out of sermons on the words of the prophet Elijah, who screamed throughout the centuries, "How long will you go limping between two opinions? If the Lord be God, then follow him." For insight we minor poets also look to the saints of our tradition, who emerge ever so rarely, not only to speak this biblical truth but also to embody it. Certainly this includes such major poets of the soul as Augustine, Gregory the Great, Thomas Aquinas, Dante, Anselm, Julian of Norwich, Luther, Jonathan Edwards, and more recently Martin Luther King Jr. and Mother Teresa. As one studies their biographies, it soon becomes obvious that, as T. S. Eliot claimed, their lives became more focused on a single great idea, and this is the deep truth that lies behind all of the words they wrote. The deep truth took over their lives. All their youthful distractions were eventually abandoned as they embodied the revelation of a particular mystery. Mother Teresa could not have spoken about the beauty of the poor without becoming poor any more than the Apostle Paul could have described justification by faith without himself abandoning other hopes for making life right again.

This means that major poets did not live well-balanced lives. Typically, they made lousy spouses, if they bothered to marry at all, and they had little time for hobbies, experimentation, recreation, or social lives. There are certainly exceptions, but most of them wouldn't do particularly well at dinner parties. (It's impossible to imagine a pleasant conversation with John the Baptist in the coffee hour following worship.) Living extreme lives was simply one of the costs of their calling as major poets. But there was no other way for them to live — they were possessed by the poetry.

No major poet ever lived to see what happened to the holy mystery they proclaimed. Occasionally, on their deathbeds, they give us a glimpse of the sadness this created, which is another cost of their holy calling. Not even the Apostle Paul knew what would happen to the struggling churches his preaching began all over the Roman Empire. It's the poetry that's eternal — not the poet.

The vast majority of pastors are not major but minor poets whose humble calling is to spend their lives making sense of the major lines of poetry they have inherited from the sacred tradition to a specific gathering of people called the local congregation. As Eliot claims, "Every people should have its own poetry."[6] But the creativity of the minor poet is found

6. T. S. Eliot, "The Social Function of Poetry," in *On Poetry and Poets*, p. 7.

not in the discovery of new truth, or in speaking and writing for every other people. It's found in the fresh articulation of familiar old truths in a specific context. Clearly, that's what pastors do.

The "minor" ingredient in the minor poet's calling does not refer to a poet of a lesser caliber. Just as St. Augustine interpreted the fall of Rome as but another chapter in the sacred drama between the City of God and the cities of earth, so the local pastor looks beneath the text of current events in the parish to discover the work of the Savior. That is no less difficult a challenge than making sense of the collapse of empires. Also, as a poet the pastor speaks in language that is neither descriptive of what is happening (the text) nor prescriptive of what should happen (the desired text), but evocative of the startling mystery God is making happen (the subtext). Not only in the sermon, but most obviously there, the pastor-poet combines words with care, believing that they can pull up the floorboards of both the biblical and the human texts. That is where the work of redemption is always found.

The minor poet knows these people. He or she knows the unique struggles, confusions, and yearnings they carry around in their hearts because they are perceived not as people in general but as the collection of individuals who have made their way into the heart of the pastor. Over the years they have invited the pastor into enough of the mystery of their lives that it is now possible for him or her to see beyond the constructed identities of smiling faces and freshly pressed dresses that fill the church's photo directory. Their pastor is theirs.

The rural pastor would never make the mistake of only preaching about the congregation's responsibility to the urban homeless.

The pastor at the old downtown First Church wouldn't think of climbing into the pulpit to offer a sermon that provides hope for the family farm.

Both pastors, however, have to be well-schooled in over two thousand years of major theological poetry in order to know the Gospel truth they preach. And they both have to hone their skills as poets in order to present that Gospel to their congregations with all of the relevance and life-overhauling power that it had when Jesus spoke to Palestinian Jews in his ancient society. Most seminaries do a much better job of training their students how to do the first thing — knowing the truth. That's what all of the courses on church history, theology, ancient languages, and biblical exegesis provide. It schools students in the major poets. But few new pastors have been trained in the exegesis of a local culture, a particular congregation, or the human soul. The legacy of this is that we are better at knowing the deep passions and pathos of dead people than the ones we have vowed to serve.

Beholding versus Believing

Without minor poets, the major poets' amazing breakthroughs into sacred mystery remain distant, objectified doctrine. Most parishioners, for example, are not unaware that we are justified before God by grace through faith. They have heard these favorite words of the church from the time they were children squirming in the pews. Few would deny the "reality" of this doctrine. But without a parish poet who can invite them into their own conflicted souls, where they encounter their serious doubts that this could possibly be "true" given the judgmental nature of life, they will never be amazed by amazing grace.

Barbara Brown Taylor has described her own breakthrough into this discovery as a pastor:

> Once I had begun crying on a regular basis, I realized just how little interest I had in defending Christian beliefs. The parts of the Christian story that had drawn me into the Church were not the believing parts but the beholding parts.
> "Behold, I bring you good news of great joy . . ."
> "Behold the Lamb of God . . ."
> "Behold, I stand at the door and knock . . ."
> Whether the narratives starred hayseed shepherds confronted by hosts of glittering angels or desert pilgrims watching something like a dove descend upon a man in a river as a voice from heaven called him "Beloved," Christian faith seemed to depend on beholding things that were clearly beyond belief. . . . While I understood both why and how the early church decided to wrap those mysteries in protective layers of orthodox belief, the beliefs never seized my heart the way the mysteries did.[7]

7. Barbara Brown Taylor, *Leaving Church: A Memoir of Faith* (San Francisco: HarperSanFrancisco, 2006), pp. 109-10.

This was one of Taylor's pivotal realizations leading her to a decision to leave pastoral ministry in a church. After years of over-functioning as the "omnicompetent" pastor of a growing church, managing the relentlessly numbing reality of the shop, attempting to meet the every need that walked through the door, rising to contradictory expectations, and teaching belief as neutrally as possible, she had no choice but to leave for the sake of her own insatiable thirst to once again "behold." It wasn't just that she was burned out. The danger was far greater than that. As she claims, "My role and my soul were eating each other alive."[8] She had entered the ministry out of passion, but after fifteen years of doing it, she found that at the end of the long day the best she could do was give God a peck on the cheek the same way she would her husband, while she was "drying up inside for want of making love."[9] She ran for her life.

I understand the decision to stop being a pastor. I even applaud it. Pastors have higher callings in life than being a pastor, and foremost among them is glorifying and enjoying God. If it's no longer possible to do that in the role of a priest, then it is certainly time to go. But it's impossible not to wonder if there is another way. What if, instead of working so hard at omnicompetence, pastors were free to work hard simply at being better poets? And is it possible that the call to parish ministry can come not at the expense of our souls, but at their delight — the joy known only by those who can behold mystery and truth at work just beneath the surface of all the belief and all the reality of parish life?

Of this, I am certain. The congregation will never ask their pastor to remain loyal to the identity of a minor poet. They need one too much to even know that they need one, as the long list of expectations and relentless efforts at reconstructing pastoral identity reveal. But that is only another reason why they need to be in church. If there they meet someone who really can help them behold, and who is believable because traces of the Shekinah are still found on the pastor's own face, eventually they'll never again settle for a realist climbing into their pulpit.

8. Taylor, *Leaving Church*, p. 111.
9. Taylor, *Leaving Church*, p. 99.

CHAPTER 3

The Unpoetic Congregation

I was still twenty feet away from the fellowship hall when the scent of the overcooked lasagna met me. The conversation with the Strattons went too long. (Maybe I can call Ted Lambert tomorrow. And don't forget Mr. Jefferson in the hospital.) By the time I arrived for the church supper, the place was already bustling. The older women were hovering over the long tables, rearranging each other's salads and desserts to make room for one more. The main dish, prepared in the church's kitchen, was enthroned in the middle surrounded by heavily buttered slices of French bread nestled in gingham paper napkins and small wicker baskets. The thermoses filled with iced tea and lemonade had already begun to leak onto the stained floor. And the children were omnipresent. Their parents, while continuing conversations with friends at the table, kept telling the kids to sit down and finish eating.

I stood at the door of this all-too-familiar scene and wondered how many times I had done this. How many meals had I eaten on metal folding chairs? How many photos of grandchildren had I admired in this room? Time to dive in again. But I couldn't just grab some food and sit down as if I were simply a part of this crowd. My job, here, was to butterfly around a bit.

"Hi, John, how are those new rosebushes coming along?" "Sally, you did a great job with that announcement last Sunday." "Bill, when are you going to give me a ride in that new Beemer?" "Mary, I tried to see your husband in the hospital this morning, but I was running a little late. . . ."

WHEN I WAS A YOUNG PASTOR, this was the part of the job that I just hated. All of the glad-handed chatting made me feel like a church politician gathering up cheap votes. And there was so much of it, not only in the fellowship hall but also in the narthex, in the corridors, around the office, and certainly in the homes where I was invited for dinner. A little small talk was even the inevitable warm-up act for every counseling appointment. And I had learned all that deep theology.

As an introvert, chatting has never come easily for me. But eventually I figured out that it is not so much a gift as a skill that anyone can learn. I still don't enjoy it very much, but a time came when I discovered that not only could I do it, but I needed to do it. It's as important to the American pastor as learning Swahili is to the East African missionary. This is the language of comfort in our society, and it simply isn't possible to proclaim the Gospel without honoring it. The most significant turning point in my attitude about chatting, however, came when I learned how to listen through it.

I began pastoral ministry prepared to enter into the depths of human pathos or to climb to the mountaintops of praise and gratitude with my parishioners. I knew how to do that. But no one in seminary taught me how to walk around in the flat plains of routine conversations about ordinary things, which is where the vast majority of my parishioners spend their days. The mistake I made during those early years was assuming that if people weren't in crisis, then I had little to offer them with all of my new reflective listening skills and profound insights about the Savior who descends even into hell to find the lost. What the congregation taught me was that among the greatest of human thirsts is to find God in the routine, even though we are so ambivalent about encountering holiness that we use the routine to excuse ourselves from the meeting. "Nothing special going on here," we say. "Don't need God for this one."

We wrap ourselves in small talk about small things in order to hide from holiness. All of the chatter about things that everyone knows do not really matter is nothing more than fig leaves we use to cloak the naked truth of who we are and what we have done to the holy garden we were given. Who we are is less than we were created to be, and what we have done is to lose the sacred in the ordinary. The garden that was meant to be a daily experience of holiness is now just a garden. In our souls we know we were created to see more, but we have no way of restoring what we've lost. So we attempt to find an excuse to wash our hands of the whole business of holiness by relegating ourselves to small things we think are unimportant to God but with which we have some success. "Nice job on the rosebushes." I might as well have said, "Very impressive fig leaves." But the human soul will relentlessly seek the sacred because it belongs to God, and is always looking for its home even though it fears that it will be judged if it gets there. As Rudolf Otto has explained, we are both drawn to God and terrified of holy encounters at the same time.[1] This holy ambivalence is what compels us to cloak life in common anonymity, but we cannot rest with that. From a place deep inside persists the yearning to find an eternity of significance to life.

It is for this reason that people come to church these days, which means that it now falls to their pastors to help them find sacred poetry for lives that only appear unpoetic. The only way to do this is to peel back the veneer of the ordinary to reveal holiness. That can never be done well, however, unless the pastor enters the ordinary to appreciate and share it as a sacramental experience of God.

It is not helpful, and certainly not redemptive, for me to sweep away all the small talk too quickly and insist that we only talk in theological language while I'm passing the butter at a church dinner. Not only is that annoying; more significantly, it misses the point. My job is not to create a community of Gnostics who have turned their spiritual backs on the concerns of the material world. To the contrary, my calling is to help them find the spirituality of the material. Even the fig leaves belong to God. I cannot help them see that without first enjoying the very real, material things that they spend their lives fretting over. The reason I enjoy the ordinary and invite others to enjoy it is that it contains portals which invite us to experience the holiness that lies just beneath all creation.

Poetry for Small Things

The nineteenth-century materialistic philosopher Ludwig Feuerbach will always be remembered for claiming, "A man is what he eats."[2] With this statement, he was criticizing all affirmations about what we would now call the spiritual life. We are just material beings, he believed. Life consists

---

1. Rudolf Otto, *The Idea of the Holy* (London: Oxford University Press, 1923).
2. Wilhelm Bolin and Friedrich Jodl, *Ludwig Feuerbach's Samtliche Werke* (Stuttgart, 1903-11), vol. 10, pp. 3-24.

only of what we make of it with whatever amount of rationality, love, and joy we can find on our own without any recourse to God. "Truth, reality, and sensation are identical," he wrote.[3] This means that there is no sacred subtext in life, no poetic mystery, no idealism. There isn't even a soul. We are what we eat; there's nothing else inside of us.

The Orthodox theologian Alexander Schmemann uses the same words as Feuerbach to make a compelling call to embrace all of life as sacred.[4] Schmemann agrees that we are what we eat, but believes that this is precisely what makes us spiritual. The biblical interpretation of life begins with the affirmation that we were created hungry, and the whole world is our food. With the exception of one tree, everything else in the garden was given to us as means of enjoying the Creator. Only as we take in the world, with reverence and gratitude, do we fulfill our created destiny to embrace God.

It is amazing how much of the biblical story involves eating. It starts with the creation of a hungry man and woman and ends with a messianic banquet. In the Old Testament, covenants are sealed with meals. Good and bad choices are made over food, whether it be a bowl of porridge or a great banquet. And it is by eating the Passover Seder that the Hebrews remember God's deliverance. In the New Testament, Jesus performs his first miracle at a wedding reception, feeds thousands of people, establishes his sacrament of grace at the Last Supper, and is revealed to travelers with the breaking of bread. Even the first-church squabble is over the Gentile widows being left out of the distribution of bread.

Clearly, the biblical depiction of humanity is that we are created hungry, but eating is so much more than mere fuel for our material bodies. It is one of the means by which the holy drama of our lives is played out. As Schmemann continues,

> In the Bible, the food that man eats, the world of which he must partake in order to live, is given to him by God, and it is given as communion with God. The world as man's food is not something "material" and limited to material functions, thus different from, and

3. Ludwig Feuerbach, *Principles of the Philosophy of the Future*, trans. Manfred Vogel (Indianapolis: Hackett Publishing Co., 1986), p. 51.

4. Alexander Schmemann, *For the Life of the World* (Crestwood, N.Y.: St. Vladimir's Seminary Press, 2000), p. 11.

opposed to, the specifically "spiritual" functions by which man is related to God.[5]

God gave us food, the most basic material need of life. That means it's a blessing. To call it a blessing is to claim that it is a means for knowing God. This is why we teach our children to bow their heads and say a prayer of thanks before the family eats. In those little prayers before the meal, we are reminding ourselves that even eating is a means of having communion with God. We do that because our real hunger is for the giver of the blessed food, and we can know this God even in the most ordinary material act of sitting down to a dish of overcooked lasagna.

As a pastor, I have discovered that most of the people who come to church would say that they agree with Schmemann, but they function as if Feuerbach is right. It's just another lasagna. But that's why I'm there — I'm the parish poet who helps them pay attention to the significance of their beliefs. The first thing I have to do, though, is to participate in the materiality of their eating, their running around, and their small talk about small concerns. But if I ever see these things apart from their sacred origins, then I too am functioning as if "truth, reality, and sensation are identical." My calling is to insist, for them, that truth is never limited to reality and sensations, but is also never far away. The only way to do that, the only way the Bible does it, is to provide poetry to the unpoetic. It's never just lasagna.

I grew up with a fabulously large grandmother who was convinced that eating was the cure to every problem in life. It didn't matter if I was in grief over the loss of a baseball game, or if I had broken my nose, she would always put some more food in front of me and say, "Honey, you just need to eat something." Somehow, it always helped. Of course, there is little that food is going to do for a broken bone or even a broken heart, but the love she served up with every dish had an amazing ability to heal whatever I brought to her kitchen table. Most people would readily admit that their best memories in life usually involved sitting at someone's table. Even when we eat alone, we have only to return to that childhood lesson of saying the blessing in order to turn a solitary meal into holy communion. This is what Solomon meant when he told us, "Eat your bread with enjoyment, and drink your wine with a merry heart; for God has long ago approved what you do" (Eccles. 9:7). Yes, God approved of eating and drinking at

5. Schmemann, *For the Life of the World,* p. 14.

creation because it was always meant to be a means of tasting sacredness, and that leaves the heart merry.

It is striking that our fall from Paradise also revolved around food. There was only the fruit of one tree that we were not given by God. It was not blessed, and not provided as a means of communion with sacred love. To eat of this fruit, therefore, was to seek food for its own end. Adam and Eve's reach for it symbolizes our striving to make work, family, health, or money their own ends. This, then, is our original sin. That old doctrine of the church refers not just to our primal disobedience to God's command. It also means that by seeking the fruit of the garden for its own sake, we have pulled the spiritual out of it and made the world material. It's not only our original sin; it's our continued addiction.

Sin is anything that separates us from God — or, to put it another way, sin is an effort to separate God from the part of creation we are holding. According to the Apostle Paul, the wages of sin is death (Rom. 6:23) — spiritual death. That's why we live in a society filled with people who have so much but whose spirits have withered. It's why they try to content themselves with frenzied activity about things that they know are not worthy of their lives. It's why the talk is small. It's because they cannot find life-giving holiness in any of it. But in their souls the old longing persists to find eternity in the small things that make up a life. And that's why they need a pastor.

To be faithful to the calling, then, the pastor has to know how to serve as a minor poet who peers beneath the most ordinary routine to find spirituality reconciled to materiality. For as the major poetry claims, in Christ God has reconciled all things (Col. 1:15-20). That accounts for everything, including chitchat at church dinners and any other small thing of life that distracts us from the sacred mystery of life.

Poetry for the Rationally Crazed

One of the greatest challenges the minor poet encounters is bidding parishioners to join in the search for mystery beneath the surface of the ordinary. They are often resistant to dropping their fig leaves in order to live in the open vulnerability of life before their Creator — not only because they feel guilty about making the garden material, but also because they are simply unaccustomed to living with sacred mystery. Our culture has functioned too long with reasonable explanations and without holy stories or wondrous mythologies. We now assume that we made it through another day because our bodies were still working, there was food in the refrigerator, and we had enough money to pay most of our bills. But all of these explanations appeal only to other ordinary phenomena and make no reference to the ideals or the beauty that lie behind them. As G. K. Chesterton has reminded us, the sun rises every morning not only because of the natural laws of science, but because like a small child, God squeals with delight over routine and tells the sun to "do it again."[6] That is what the soul needs to hear in order to find any delight for itself in the routines of another new day.

Ironically, it's a vision of the mystery beneath the rational that keeps us reasonable. This is why Chesterton also claimed, "Poets do not go mad; but chess players do. . . . Poetry is sane because it floats easily in an infinite sea; reason seeks to cross the infinite sea, and so make it finite. The result is mental exhaustion."[7] Chesterton's point is that everything can be understood by what is not understood. It is also the point of mysticism, spirituality, theology, the Bible, and even Archimedes. We are able to make sense of what we see only by finding our way to something that is just beyond the world that is known. Poets believe this, but most people were trained to see the world as a chess game in which the goal is to make all the right strategic moves with the hopes of winning, whatever that may mean.

For example, a single mother wakes up one morning thinking only about how much work she has to accomplish at the office. But before she even gets dressed, her seven-year-old son begins to complain about a sore throat. She begins her first argument of the day by asking him, "Just how sore is it, really?" After his continued protests, she checks in his mouth and realizes that he's not going to be able to go to school. So she quickly burns through her entire list of babysitters before finally talking someone into watching him. By then, she's late for her first appointment at the office, which leads to a scolding from her boss. That leaves her grumpy enough to start an argument with her secretary, who had nothing to do with the boy's sore throat. It isn't even ten A.M., and her whole day is already consumed by an irrational chaos of successive arguments, which are really all variations on her basic struggle to make the day work out well.

6. G. K. Chesterton, *Orthodoxy* (Colorado Springs: Waterbrook Press, 1994), p. 61.

7. Chesterton, *Orthodoxy,* pp. 12-13.

Should this woman stumble into church after a week of this frustration, she is not going to be accustomed to hearing that there is any sacred mystery to her life. She may be hoping that her pastor will provide more tips or strategies for holding together the competing demands on her life. Worse yet, she may come to church seeking only some spiritual entertainment that will distract her from the insanity of her week. But what she really needs is a vision of the holiness of her life, as uncontrollable as it will always be.

The pastor who wants to offer this grace begins by inviting the congregation to remember the old yearnings for beauty, delight, and wild adventure. These are the marks of life known by those who are living sanely, and it would be crazy to keep collecting days without them. Recovering such a passionate life is the work of the Savior, Jesus Christ, and it's one of the reasons why we call him a savior. But describing that life is the work of poets. Every time the pastor is given the opportunity to move from small talk to poetry — through pastoral care, counseling, devotionals, and sermons — he or she doesn't simply quote Scripture. As a minor poet, the pastor has to maintain both sides of the conversation between God and the people. If the pastor only presents biblical words to the congregation, the holy conversation succumbs to a one-sided lecture. It's even questionable if the lecture is still holy, since everything that has been revealed about holiness depicts it as communion with God. This means that the congregation must recognize not only God's words to them but also their own insatiable thirst for those words. And so the minor poet always finds a way to express sublimated longings, longings that have become inaccessible because we easily lose touch with them in a world of chess players.

Simply by freeing these old yearnings for a sane and yet more passionate way of life, the poet has already been of inestimable help in the work of transformation. T. S. Eliot has written, "In expressing what other people feel, [the poet] is also changing the feeling by making it more conscious; he is making people more aware of what they feel already, and therefore teaching them something about themselves."[8] Through consciousness the feeling is changed not by becoming different but by becoming powerful. Once the truth of our souls is spoken and placed beside the life-giving response of God's truth, the holy conversation is carried on by the Holy Spirit, who does the work of bringing people back to life. This is why po-

---

8. T. S. Eliot, "The Social Function of Poetry," in *On Poetry and Poets* (New York: Farrar, Straus & Cudahy, 1957), p. 9.

36

etry does not have to be defended, inculcated, or coerced. It only appears defenseless. Its power resides not in the orthodoxy of the verse, and certainly not in the creativity of the poet, but in the inspired word that has the power to untangle the distorted image of God. The truth of holy poetry is buoyant. It will rise to the surface to do all the convicting and compelling once it is freed simply through expression.

As pastors we provide this liberating service not only by devoting a portion of our sermons to the people's half of the sacred conversation, but also by offering prayers that express to God what has been impatiently waiting in the souls of the congregation. Pastor-poets avoid manipulating these prayers into didactic instruction about what we ought to do, and never use phrases that begin with such words as "Teach us that. . . ." Instead, we simply pray. Our words rise from the bottom of our congregants' souls. By the end of the prayer, others in the room are thinking, "Yes, that is what I wanted to say but didn't know how."

As with all poetry, through prayer the truth is out, and it has set us free. We have confessed that no matter how strategic we are, we are not winning the chess game. If there is a gospel for us, it is going to have to sweep up all the pieces of life, especially the small pawns, into a far more dramatic adventure. In this better drama it's not the reasoned strategies that save us, but the confession that we are filled with yearning to be fully alive.

One Saturday morning as I was running on a trail that wound through a neighborhood park, a group of boys from two college cross-country teams flew past me. Their bodies were sleek and strong. They wore uniforms that made them all look like Olympians. And they were so fast that I began to feel like a lumbering truck that wasn't going to make it up the hill. About the time I had recovered from this indignity, the girls' team raced past me with all of the grace and speed of gazelles. When I finally got to the end of the trail, all of the real runners were long done and were talking with their coaches. And there I was, doubled over, sucking wind, and telling myself that there's no such thing as a good run.

As I slunk away from the crowd toward my car, I noticed another group of runners starting to reach the end of the trail. This group had no fancy uniforms. They wore baggy gym shorts and T-shirts with something hastily scrawled across them. A few were running hard, but most had a clumsy pace. The cross-country teams immediately moved back to the finish line and began cheering wildly as each of these last runners stumbled to the end. Curious, I went over to get a closer look and noticed that this last group of runners were all developmentally disabled. Some of them had very obvious handicaps, but still they ran. They had no interest in the coaches' clipboards and stopwatches, and they seemed oblivious to the fact that this was a race. They were running with abandon for the sheer delight of it. A few were being pushed in wheelchairs. Then two girls who had Down syndrome appeared at the end, walking, holding hands, smiling and waving to those of us who clapped and kept on clapping. No one cheered more loudly than I. And when I got back to my car, I couldn't stop crying.

Why were we all cheering so enthusiastically for these kids with handicaps? Maybe it was because we were proud of their resolve not to be limited. Maybe. But a poet would wonder if there is something in all of us, something essentially human, that envies those who are graced with the opportunity to live without veneer. They certainly knew more than I did about the joy of running in a park on a crisp fall morning.

Joy cannot be analyzed, strategized, or explained. It can only be entered, and the portal into joy is confessing the truth: We are not whole. No one has to pretend, and the truth feels so good that we just want to cheer whenever someone exhibits it.

Poetry for the Angry

The Reformers claimed that the church would always be a hospital for sinners. This means that we cannot expect its members to be spiritually healthy. But neither can we protect ourselves from the unhealthy any more than a doctor can stay away from a hospital just because it's filled with sick people. The reason people need pastors is precisely because someone has to show them how to find healing for the sin-sick soul that knows so little joy.

The primary symptom of a soul that has become sick is that it becomes blind to the poetry of life. This is not only because it can no longer see the beauty of the small miracles that fill a day, or that it has become so crazed with strategies that it can no longer enjoy the mystery of life's unfolding drama, but also because the soul has settled into its disappointments, which has left it angry.

The Apostle Paul cautions us, "Be angry but do not sin" (Eph. 4:26). What this implies is that it isn't the anger that separates us from God, and that it's possible to be "good and mad," as the old saying goes. Much of the major poetry of Scripture illustrates the righteous anger of both humans and God, who are usually mad at each other. The reason they're angry is that one feels abandoned by the other, and the reason the anger is righteous is that they tell each other what they feel, which means it is still a form of holy communion. God has good self-esteem and can handle as much anger as we can dish out, as the psalmists apparently believed, but it's clear that nothing infuriates God more than being left out of the conversation.

What hurts our souls is when we gorge ourselves on anger, at God or other people, until it makes us sick. Anything that tastes as good as anger should be taken in moderation and never on an empty stomach. But the problem with anger is that it makes us lose interest in the blessings of life because we can only think about the one infuriating thing. We obsess over it and become intoxicated with the hurt we feel. This is why the old saints claimed that victimization is a waste of our suffering. Once we take on the identity of victims, we are allowing nothing redemptive to occur, and since we have idolized the anger, how can we be open to such divine gifts as healing, forgiveness, and the gravitas that emerges through adversity?

This is not to say that there are not victims, but no one has to make that the defining mark of their identity. In the words of concentration-camp survivor Viktor Frankl, "The last of the human freedoms is to determine our response. . . . In the final analysis it becomes clear that the sort of person a prisoner became was the result of an inner decision, and not the result of the camp influences alone."[9] Getting to that critical inner decision is tricky. But churches are filled with people who need help in making this inner decision to stop focusing on the "camp influences" and to define life by something other than disappointment, anger, and thus victimization.

It is the minor poets who get to see human lives being reshaped by the holy mysteries introduced to us by the major poets. It takes time — a lot of time, usually — but the truth really can sculpt a life. It always amazes a pastor to witness a new creation beginning to emerge as the Holy Spirit uses the poetry in a parishioner's life, chipping away the cynicism that is manifested in becoming mean. But always from the inside out. And usually with so much subtlety that it takes a poet to find it.

Often this miracle unfolds in the very person who has been the biggest

---

9. Viktor Frankl, *Man's Search for Meaning* (New York: Simon & Schuster, 1963), pp. 104-5.

pain in the neck. On more than one occasion I have been called to the deathbed of one of the congregation's bullies. Sometimes there is a surprise waiting.

Jack Williams had resisted nearly every proposal and initiative I had developed since arriving at "his church." But he had so overplayed his hand that I soon figured out he was just resisting me. After he called me a horse's ass in a committee meeting one night, another longtime member of the church stayed behind to check on me. Trying to offer me some comfort, she gave me a big hug and said, "Jack is just that way. It wasn't personal." But it sure felt personal. Over the years of my service to that church, as I walked to the pulpit on Sunday mornings, I would see Jack sitting there, always in the fifth pew next to the side aisle on the right, with his arms crossed. Sometimes before I said a word I asked myself again, "What did I do to him?" More than once I toyed with the fantasy of just setting the carefully prepared sermon aside and saying, "All right, Jack Williams. Let's have it out right now in front of everyone else. What is it? What? What? *What?*" But I never did that. Instead, I did what I was called there to do and said, "Hear the Word of the Lord."

It had not escaped my attention that after several years he began to change. He allowed his hands to fall to his lap. He eventually stopped looking at me so sternly. Then he stopped looking at me altogether.

One night, very late, his wife woke me up with a phone call. It was obvious that she'd been crying. "We brought Jack into the emergency room a couple of hours ago," she said. "He went to bed just complaining of indigestion. But it looks like he's having a bad heart attack. He's asked for you." I remember hanging up the phone and staring at it as it sat on the nightstand. "Did I just dream that," I wondered, "or was that really Betty Williams telling me that her husband wanted me to come to him?"

It's amazing how quiet hospitals are late at night. As I walked down the stark corridors, I could hear my footsteps clipping along the freshly polished linoleum. I knew that the hopes and fears of all the years were colliding in each of the rooms I passed as patients who couldn't sleep were staring at the ceiling, wondering. . . .

I entered the ICU tentatively, almost apologetically, because I assumed that the whole family was as angry with me as Jack was. But, of course, they weren't really thinking about me at all. Betty came out of the glass room where Jack lay tied up by tubes attached to machines that measured the time he had left. She took both of my hands in hers, apologized for getting me out in the middle of the night, and thanked me too much for coming. Then she led me to Jack's bedside.

As soon as he saw me, he pushed the oxygen mask aside in spite of her protests. As he squeezed my hand, I saw the tears welling up in his eyes. I remember thinking that this was a strange place and time to get to the bottom of his anger with me. That was not what happened, though.

He just whispered, "Thank you."

Now I knew why I was there. It was the last rite Jack wanted with a pastor he didn't much like. He simply wanted to die with gratitude, not with curses on his lips. After those two profoundly hopeful words, he placed the oxygen mask back over his mouth, closed his eyes, and didn't say another word to me. I said something, I'm sure, but it was forgettable even to me. I must have prayed. What I do remember is that Jack and I were now done. The Spirit had given us both a small but extravagant gift at the end of a life, and like all of God's gifts, this one was made all the more precious by being wrapped in mystery.

When I came back the next day, Jack was in a coma. He died four days later. There would be no more words. Just a "Thank you" at the end. I would love to believe that the years of listening to sermons about gratitude for the grace of God somehow slipped their way over and under Jack's crossed arms to make their way into his head and his heart. Maybe. For a minor poet, that hope would have to be enough.

CHAPTER 4

The Poet's Pathos

The program in the fellowship hall was a visiting youth choir from Malawi that didn't appear worried about finishing on time. I thanked myself for telling the organizers of the evening that I would pray at the beginning of the program, and then mentioned to the person next to me that I had to leave for a strategic-planning committee meeting.

Of all the church committees I attend, this one makes the least sense to me. There's just something that seems a bit silly about telling God what we will get accomplished in the next five years — particularly since the great events in the congregation always show up as divine interruptions of our plans. And the terrible events — well, who can really plan for them?

The meeting was already underway by the time I entered the room. Most of the people around the table were lost in a repeated conversation about the parking lot. I noticed that everyone was engaged by the topic except Joan Lambert, who just sat there, looking straight ahead at something no one else could see. I remembered that I still needed to call her husband, Ted, who had left a message that he wanted to talk with me. I had assumed it was about the custodian because I had heard that that was the issue bothering him, but now I was wondering if something else was up.

When the meeting was over and everyone was leaving the room, I met Joan at the door and asked her if she was okay. She seemed startled by the question. Then she stepped back into the room and whispered, "I'm sorry. I probably shouldn't have come tonight, but I had to get out of the house." After a long pause she bit her lip and, abandoning the whisper, blurted out, "This morning Ted came down to the kitchen, poured a cup of coffee, and told me that he didn't love me. He's going to leave."

A very familiar knot reappeared in my stomach.

LIKE MOST PASTORS, I get to a lot of committee meetings. My ability to find meaning in them is directly related to my insistence on sitting at the table as the parish poet. Of course, I have to keep one eye on the agenda, but the other, more probing eye is constantly looking for portals into the subtext of the meeting. Anybody with a few skills can run an effective meeting, so why waste a pastor on that assignment? I'm really being paid to "mole" my way beneath the discussion in search of underlying dynamics, hidden agendas, and responses to the question "What are we really worried about?" The chances are great that this is where I will find the Gospel's agenda.

There are times when this real agenda for the meeting involves the whole committee that serves as a microcosm of Christ's unfolding drama with the congregation. But more often, lots of little diverse meetings between the Savior and individuals are going on concurrently as the dullness of the group discussion gives opportunity to the human soul to ponder its own issues. This is what I found at the meeting that night. Joan Lambert got her body to the church, but her soul was still in her kitchen, where it was buried under a world caved in by the words her husband had spoken there. My real work was about to begin.

A disaster is anything that makes us feel like the stars are falling down. That's why it is called a dis-aster. The late University of Chicago theologian Mircea Eliade claimed that all religions are centered on an axis mundi, or a sacred pole that keeps earth connected to heaven.[1] This can be a totem pole, the center pole of the tribal hut, a temple, or the cross of the Christians. Whenever there is a disaster, no matter how personal or global in scope, people rush to their axis mundi to insure that the heavens are not collapsing on top of them. If they think, for one moment, that they have been abandoned by their sacred pole, they're plunged into anomie and

---

1. Mircea Eliade, *The Sacred and the Profane* (New York: Harcourt Brace Jovanovich, 1957), p. 32.

chaos. This is why Joan Lambert was staring into nothing during our committee meeting. How could she participate in a discussion about strategic planning when one of her most sacred covenants was breaking apart? That certainly wasn't in her plan for life. For me to be of use to her as a pastor, I had to know what it felt like to enter the meaningless chaos.

The Dark Night of the Soul

After St. John of the Cross was imprisoned for the religious reforms he tried to bring to sixteenth-century Spain, he wrote a little book that has continued to guide confused Christians to this day. His point was that God "rewards" those who pray fervently with a moment in their lives when they lose everything they have spent their lives trying to gain. If they haven't physically lost what was cherished, then they've lost the meaning and hope that the cherished things used to provide. On this dark night, they have no choice but to hang on to the cross with Christ while everything else in life drops off. They think they are losing even God. But they are actually losing only their instrumental use for God. It is then that Christians answer the most important questions of their souls. Do I still want God if that comes without any additional blessings? What if it is just God, and nothing else — not marriage, health, prosperity, or any other granting of petition. Would I still love God?

One would think that those who have passed through this dark night are beaten up. They may be, but they are also rewarded with freedom because they no longer live in fear of losing anything. It's already gone. And that is why they are actually joyful. Now they hold all the blessings of life in open hands, believing that they are only temporary and will surely be taken away in time. New blessings will appear in their place, and then they too will disappear. But the soul is always held securely by the God who never lets go of us. Best of all, they now realize that the cross is the only axis mundi they need. "Yes," they respond to the Dark Night, "a God who is dying to love us is enough." That's the secret to finding true joy.

Joan Lambert had just entered this terrifying place, and she wasn't anywhere near ready to see it as her opportunity to discover the sufficiency of God's love. At this point, it would have been both cruel and ludicrous for me to even suggest that this was where her dark journey would end. She was overwhelmed and dazed, like people always are after witnessing the unimaginable. So for a while I would simply listen and reassure her that she was not separated from the love of God, who has not abandoned her. But before long, she would start looking for a miraculous intervention that would make everything okay again. She would ask God to "fix" her husband, change his heart, and make him want to come back home to her. I would join her in praying for that, and I would do all I could to encourage Ted to work through his marital issues with Joan, but I would know how this story might end. In my experience, once someone moves out of the house, it's extremely difficult to get him or her back home. Whether the marriage survives or not, my job is to stay with them, and when the time is right to turn their eyes toward the new life they will need either way.

While I do feel a responsibility to help people maintain their commitments and vows, I'm not a marriage counselor. I respect therapists too much to impersonate one. So I always make a careful referral when speaking with couples in crisis, like the Lamberts. Even if they begin the hard work through therapy, I stay with these couples because I have an equally important if not more important role to play in their lives. That role is to ensure that all of their focus is not placed on each other, on recovering what was lost, or on their dreams for their future either together or apart. I'm the pastor, which means my role is to turn their faces toward the work of redemption, not just of their marriage but, even more importantly, of their lives.

Ironically, this means that I have to keep reminding them that the only hope the marriage now has is to make it no longer necessary. As a "till death do us part" vow, it is a life-shaping covenant and the highest vocation of married people. But it only takes one person leaving to reveal that marriage is not necessary. And when couples make it to the end of their lives still hand in hand, it is because they always knew it wasn't necessary, which is exactly why they chose to do the hard work of keeping their hands together.

The secret to intimacy with another person is discovering the sufficiency of God's love without that person. It is the only way we are ever free to give love to another human being who can never meet the needs of our souls. This is why in premarital counseling all of the decent pastors I know knock themselves out to convince the couples that they cannot be Jesus for each other, which means they dare not need to get married in hopes of finding what only a Savior can provide. But when you've been married as long as Joan Lambert, assuming it was a reliable axis mundi, only to wake up one morning and hear your husband say that he's leaving, discovering God's sufficiency feels like a headlong plunge into terror.

If a pastor is going to guide parishioners through this frightening terrain, littered with the rubble of a life lost, he or she has to be familiar with it and recognize it as holy ground. This cannot be limited to a professional familiarity that allows objective distance. All poets of the soul need to have spent time themselves in this strange land where self-constructed lives are lost and the grace of new life is received. How else can we authentically be moved by our parishioners' pathos or find the authority to speak of the hopeful mercy that lies beneath their dis-asters? It isn't necessary for poets to have experienced in their own lives every tragedy that their parishioners will encounter. Of course. But it is very necessary for poets to know exactly what it feels like to have the world cave in, and then to be startled by the discovery of a resurrected life based solely on the work of Christ.

This means that parish poets have to pay attention to their own lives. They must go after their own life experiences and plunge into them in search of sacred meaning rather than run from the pain or numb themselves with busy distractions. How else can they awaken parishioners to the mystery at work within their own lives? Even if pastors have not experienced what is typically thought of as a disaster — even so, they have wandered through the dark land of loss. Even their call to ministry qualifies. They probably had other plans for life, or at least they should have had them. But a day came when they could no longer deny the constant tugging of the Holy Spirit to sacrifice the preferred plans in order to begin a journey to a place where they would rather not go. This was Jesus' prophecy to Peter in the twenty-first chapter of John's Gospel, when he spelled out the implications of tending his sheep, and it has been echoed to every shepherd of the flock of Christ since then. But the reluctant journey doesn't simply mean that the pastor has to give up a lucrative career in business or one of society's esteemed professions. More to the point, it means that the pastor has to journey into the profoundly redemptive work of Christ in his or her own ordinary losses in life. This is why we get knots in our stomachs every time parishioners tell us about their own losses. We know what this feels like. We may even be the only person they know who understands what is really at stake in their experience. And we are moved by the pathos of the story they tell, no matter how great or insignificant it appears on the surface.

As poets, pastors aren't afforded the luxury of skimming over the top of their own losses, thinking, "That was no big deal." The big deal is learning how to dig through loss to find the hints of hope — not a cheery optimism, but deep, from-the-bottom-of-the-soul hope. After years of excavation through their own losses, pastors learn how to find this sacred subtext in others. There is no other way for us to believe authentically that dawn will come for a parishioner's dark night. When the sheep of our flock are in the midst of their frightening losses, they need to lean upon our faith and our trust that they are not abandoned to this destruction. They need to believe that at least we believe.

Cardinal Leo Joseph Suenens, the late prelate of Brussels, was known to whisper something into the ears of new priests at their ordination ceremonies: "Remember, God has called you to the priesthood because he does not trust you to be a layman." Anyone who's spent thirty minutes in the pastorate knows exactly what the old cardinal meant. We have to pray. We pray not only for the sake of our own souls, but also for those who look into our souls to find God.

Gravitas

Even the most cursory reading of Scripture reveals that God is not easy on those called into ministry. It even seems as though some get overused in the biblical drama. By the end of their lives, Abraham, Moses, David, all of the prophets, Paul, and all of the disciples were scarred over from their wounds. The apostles had been kicked out of most of the towns in the Roman Empire, often with a shower of stones behind them. At the end, when Paul was imprisoned and presumably executed in Rome, the success of his life's work in founding churches was hardly secure. But all he really wanted to write about in his prison epistles was the surpassing joy of great worth he had discovered. There isn't a single battered leader in the Scriptures who would have opted out of the story simply because it costs so much to be used by God. That's because they all had discovered Paul's surpassing joy. How did they do that? By paying attention to holy drama within their own souls, which was the only way they could be of sacred use to the people they were called to serve.

There is no easy way to find this drama, however. It doesn't come from the pastor's library, seminary education, con-ed seminars, or a new building program. After trying all of this, the pastor is left only with having to attend to the quiet joy that lies beneath the pathos of his or her own story with Christ. Everything else informs and interprets this. If it isn't true for the pastor, why should anyone else believe the Gospel the pastor proclaims?

The old seminary professors used to speak about a necessary trait for pastoral ministry called gravitas. It refers to a soul that has developed enough spiritual mass to be attractive, like gravity. It makes the soul appear old, but gravitas has nothing to do with age. It has everything to do with wounds that have healed well, failures that have been redeemed, sins that have been forgiven, and thorns that have settled into the flesh. These severe experiences with life expand the soul until it appears larger than the body that contains it. Then it is large enough to proclaim a holy joy, which is what makes the pastor's soul so attractive. The early church found gravitas through persecution. The desert fathers and monks found it by abandoning comfort and dedicating themselves to a vocation of prayer for the world. Most reformers have found it in prison. The American slaves found it in the hot cotton fields. Pastors find it by committing themselves to the One who called them into ministry, but whose work is so often resisted by the congregation and by the pastors themselves.

Gravitas sounds difficult. It is. But the only alternative is to give up on the sacred poetry, and that's the last thing a congregation needs from its pastor.

As odd as it may sound, it's the scars on the pastor's soul that make it attractive. This is also what gives credibility to the Gospel the pastor proclaims. Parishioners will always measure that credibility by the degree to which it has clearly been at work in the pastor's life. But while a scarred soul is attractive, gaping wounds are not. No congregation finds a bleeding preacher very poetic. What we pastors present with our lives is an incarnated version of the healing and redemptive work of the Gospel. This doesn't mean that we have to keep parading our own stories about. We simply speak to our congregants as a people who have existential knowledge of the truth. Everyone knows when we're speaking from our souls and not just the textbooks we've collected.

Pastors develop gravitas through many sources. I'll describe just a few of them.

Sometimes it's inherited from family. This is most evident when the pastor comes from a family whose dysfunctions are obvious. Those who were not loved well as children, because they were raised by parents too hurt to pass on anything but hurt, will often speak about the surpassing joy of a Savior dying to love them. There is a use for everything, and the reflective pastor knows this better than anyone else. God does not start being redemptive on the day that the pastor is ordained. All of the failures, hurts, and losses that occurred even in childhood are embraced by the calling into ministry. After his conversion, St. Augustine discovers that the Christ he now confesses as Lord has long been at work in his life. He prays, "See how I have explored the vast field of my memory in search of you, O Lord! And I have not found you outside it."[2] This, again, is why the pastoral knot in the stomach is so familiar. In the midst of every thick conversation with a parishioner we remember the holy drama played out in our own lives — how we thought we were abandoned to our hurts, only to discover later that the crucified Christ was there, bearing the pain with us. We were not alone.

Until we discover that Christ was not outside the collected wounds of the family that raised us, we'll never have anything to say about the wounds of the family of faith. If nothing else, the pastor raised in a dysfunctional home has the blessing of not being surprised by the crazy and self-destructive activity of the church. As the biblical drama indicates, God even seems to have a preference for working with families that are a bit messed up. Perhaps that is because they best illustrate the miraculous possibilities of redemption.

Gravitas can also be inherited from relatively healthy families who simply tell their stories well. The southern novelist Flannery O'Connor once claimed that anyone who pays attention to his or her childhood could write novels for the rest of his or her life. Again, she was referring not just to those whose family lives are tragic, but also to those who simply keep listening to the profound moments of their childhood.

Marilynne Robinson has provided a compelling illustration of this in her story about an old pastor's memory of a day from his boyhood when he received an ashen biscuit from his father on a rainy day. The adults were tearing down a church that had burned after a lightning strike, while the children were hiding from the rain under a wagon parked nearby. The boy's father came over to the wagon and handed him the biscuit wrapped in soot, saying, "Never mind, there's nothing cleaner than ash." In his old age, the pastor remembers that ashen biscuit as the bread of affliction. Every time he celebrates communion this memory returns, and he ponders an old phrase from his childhood — "Strange are the uses of adversity." As the reflective pastor writes letters to his own son, he claims, "Grief itself often returned me to that morning when I took communion from my fa-

---

2. St. Augustine, *Confessions*, trans. R. S. Pine-Coffin (London: Penguin Books, 1961), X.24, p. 230.

ther's hand."[3] So he knows about adversity simply by paying attention to the powerful, inherited symbols of his healthy family. Precious memories of a crowded Thanksgiving table, a family gathered in the pews for Christmas Eve services, or a Father who said, "You are my beloved, and with you I am so pleased" — these can provide the same legacy in a pastor's understanding of the Gospel.

The church will also produce gravitas for the pastor. Sometimes this comes from the wounds inflicted by cruel parishioners who are furious that the pastor has not provided what they want from the church. They have learned to "do whatever it takes" to get what they need from the system, and they view the pastor as only a means to their ends. Often what it takes is picking up the phone and telling someone, "I'm worried about our new minister." At other times the wounds come from transference — the pastor reminds a parishioner of a child, an ex-spouse, a boss, or a parent who was the source of unresolved hurts. These victims began to despise the pastor simply because of the photograph they saw in the brochure that the search committee mailed to the congregation. And over the course of the pastor's ministry, they'll find a legion of opportunities to retaliate in anger for what someone else did to them.

Most of the congregational wounds in a pastor's life come simply from the institutional demands of the job. Every night the pastor will drive home from another church meeting feeling depleted from the challenges of managing an organization, not at all confident that the day was spent fulfilling the calling to be of service to the work of Christ in human lives. This busyness wounds the very nature of calling. By the time the pastor pulls into the driveway at home, thoughts of abandoning the ministry are irresistible, but there's no time to process these hurts because a child is waiting for a bedtime story. So the pastor stuffs the feelings into some compartment deep inside where five-year-olds cannot find them. That only makes the wounds private, which are the most dangerous kind. Only scarred-over wounds contribute to gravitas in a pastor's soul; there are no healing scars for the hurts that continue to fester in secrecy.

Yet another type of gravitas-creating wound is the potentially fatal flaw that exists in every pastor's life. This wound comes not from the failures of either the pastor or the parishioner but from the created package of life. None of us is created whole and complete. The creation narratives make it

3. Marilynne Robinson, *Gilead* (New York: Farrar, Straus & Giroux, 2004), pp. 94-96.

clear that something is missing and forbidden in every created garden. Faithfulness means choosing to love and serve God in spite of not having everything we want. Pastors are not exempt from this created design, and like everyone else they spend their lives making choices about how they will respond to this thing that is missing from life. For some, the created wound is that they will never be married. For others it is that they will never be as healthy as they wish. Still others will continually be tempted to focus on the father or mother who could never express unconditional love. Many pastors will always wonder why they were not destined to lead a large, "successful" congregation.

Sometimes the created flaw is the pastor's lack of gifts for an esteemed component of the job description. We are not all great preachers, administrators, counselors, or extroverts with a gift for gab in the halls of the church. We may work very hard to develop skills in these areas, but they will never be gifted areas of our ministry. And that hurts. It hurts not just because we know it's what the congregation wants, but also because it is what we want for ourselves. Writing in the sixth century, Pope Gregory the Great claimed,

> For Almighty God perfects in great measure the minds of those who [lead], but leaves them partially imperfect, for this reason, that when they are resplendent with extraordinary attainments, they may grieve with disgust for their imperfections, and, least of all, exalt themselves for great things, when they have to labor and struggle against very small matters. And as they are not able to overcome the very little things, they should not presume to pride themselves on the great things they accomplish.[4]

God alone is whole and complete, lacking in nothing. So it only makes sense that those who have devoted their lives to talking about God would have at least a "small matter" that is missing, imperfect, or habitually humbling. The purpose of this unwanted — but divine — gift is to nurture even more gravitas in the pastor's soul. Such gravity is strangely attractive to a society that has tried too long to lack nothing.

These flaws uncover layers of character. Nobody really wants a perfect

---

4. Gregory the Great, *Pastoral Care*, Ancient Christian Writers: The Works of The Fathers in Translation, trans. Henry Davis, S.J. (New York: Newman Press, 1950), p. 237.

pastor. Those who sit in the pews may try to turn the pulpit into a pedestal, but that is only a projection of their own flawed aspirations to rise above their creaturely limitations. While there are certainly appropriate standards of faithfulness for leaders, what parishioners really want is a pastor who knows what it means to struggle against temptation and despair, like they do. They want to be led by someone who has also stayed up all night fretting over choices, regrets, and fear, but who then found the quiet grace to start over the next morning. They want to see the Gospel incarnated in a human life that is still far from complete but has become more interesting because the human drama is now sacred. In other words, they want a pastor who knows what it means to be them, but them in communion with God. Innocence is precious, but it's the glimpses of redemption that truly compel.

Souls Hanging Out

I find that my seminary students worry about being role models more than anything else. I tell them that, of course, they are role models. Pastors live very visible lives. Everyone in my congregation knows where I live, vacation, shop, and eat out. They know what my wife wears to church and to the grocery store, what my kids have done recently, and what kind of car I drive. They are particularly aware if I get a new car. But this fishbowl existence is not really a big deal. Either pastors get used to that quickly, or they get out of the ministry. What I try to explain to my students is that the much harder challenge is to maintain a spiritual visibility. Five minutes into the sermon on Sundays, everyone can tell if God and I are getting along okay.

A church I used to serve hired a new associate pastor, fresh from the seminary, who was bothered that everyone could watch her worshiping in the chancel on Sunday mornings. "It just creeps me out," she told me, and she asked if she could sit in the first pew until the time came for her contributions to the liturgy. I understood both the lament and the longing for a more protected place to worship. But of course I couldn't let her hide in the pew, not only because part of her job was to be a worship leader, but more importantly because she now had to learn something the seminary couldn't teach her: how to lose spiritual anonymity.

Most pastors readily admit that they envy their parishioners on Sundays. When we look across the pulpit into the pews, we remember that just about everyone else in the room, except some of the teenagers, has chosen to be there. So their worship begins in freedom, and it will continue in freedom through the hour. Even the arrangement of the furniture in a typical sanctuary protects the privacy of the pew-sitters' souls. If some of them need to spend the whole hour wearing a scowl because they and God are clearly not getting along very well, few people will notice. Or if the choral music pries its way into a protected, tender place in their hearts, it will really be just fine if some tears slide down in response. That's what a pastor envies. When we lead worship in front of all this, our souls are hanging out for all to see. We may also scowl or tear up, and we're certainly allowed, but when the service is over, we'd better be ready to talk about it at the church doors.

The same spiritual visibility is evident in more subtle forms throughout the week. A pastor drives away from a hospital wondering why a teenage girl is dying of cancer. Soon he finds that the prayer for healing he began in the hospital room is staying with him through the remaining appointments of the day. His secretary, counselees, committee members, and wife all notice his burdened countenance and ask him if he's okay. He may tell some of them what is on his heart and ask them to pray as well for the girl. This parish poet could be stuck with her in his soul for a very long time as he ponders, petitions, and digs around to find enough grace to make the burden bearable. But this is not simply between him and God. It's his job to carry the pathos around the church until it settles into the parishioners' souls as well.

The pastor's soul is even more vulnerable when it is clear that she or he has been leading the church in the wrong direction. There may be elders or other lay leaders who will share in the blame, but it's always the pastor who has to own the failure publicly. On more than one occasion I've stood in front of a congregation to say, "This project that we have been pursuing, the one that I said we just had to do — well, it isn't working. I thought this is what God wanted for us, but clearly I was wrong about that. I'm sorry." It's hard for pastors to say this because it means not only that we made a mistake, but also that we got the poetry wrong. Something was forced and thus fell out of the rhythm of God's sonnet for the congregation. And this is what the pastor is supposed to be good at. It's the reason that so much time is spent in the study. And worst of all, it reveals that there's a personal agenda lurking in the pastor's soul that has been smuggled into the poetry. Still, every time I've told a congregation that I got it wrong, they have responded to the confession with relief and overwhelming grace. One time they even applauded. Usually a wise old leader of the church will take me aside afterwards and say something like, "Hey, don't worry about it. Giving grace is supposed to be our business here." It's almost comical when I as the pastor miss the church's capacity for this.

The time when the poetic soul feels most vulnerable is when the failure is in the pastor's own life. This is also when it is hardest for the congregation to bestow the sacred grace that the pastor has been preaching week after week. Sometimes that is because the congregation believes this is a personal matter and they don't want to pry. So they say nothing about the pastor's teenage son who was arrested for drunk driving, the car that was repossessed, or the marriage that is falling apart. But this protection of privacy only prevents them from offering the grace of the Gospel. More often, churches are graceless because their members become more focused on hearing titillating gossip than on offering anything remotely redemptive to their pastor in a time of crisis. But I know from very personal experience that some congregations handle their pastor's crises with so much grace that it seems they are, in fact, the Body of Christ.

When pastors fail at living out of the Gospel that they have vowed to proclaim not only from the pulpit but also in life, it's because something in their poetic soul is disconnected from its own poetry. Usually this happens because pastors have slid into the role of professional poet. We may even think that we are being heroic by caring for the needs of the church while our own souls are drying up. But there's nothing heroic about self-destructing in front of a congregation. When Henri Nouwen checked himself into a Trappist monastery for seven months, it was because he had spent so much time writing lectures on prayer that he didn't have time to pray. And yet while complaining about all the demands on his schedule, he paradoxically found himself afraid to be alone. Eventually he came to an important realization:

> I started to see how much I had fallen in love with my own compulsions and illusions, and how much I needed to step back and wonder, "Is there a quiet stream underneath the fluctuating affirmations and rejections of my little world? Is there a still point where my life is anchored and from which I can reach out with hope and courage and confidence?"[5]

5. Henri Nouwen, *The Genesee Diary: Report from a Trappist Monastery* (Garden City, N.Y.: Image Books, 1976), p. 14.

Most pastors who come to this same discovery are not able to check themselves into a monastery for an extended stay. Some are given the glorious luxury of sabbaticals. But most either have to leave and go to another church, which does nothing for their arid souls, or struggle to re-orient their lives around the quiet stream while continuing to function in leadership, which is almost impossible. It is when the pastor feels stuck that he or she begins to self-destruct from the inside out. It's the only path left to the soul that will not be ignored for long.

The early signs of this internal crisis are really no different for pastors than they are for the parishioners whom the pastors are busily serving. As a professor of ministry, I am often asked, "How do we prevent clergy from getting into trouble?" There's no silver bullet. Pastors simply have to do the very things they call their congregations to do. Long before they sink into a spiritual crisis, they make hundreds of little decisions against their souls. They let their spiritual disciplines slip. They miss too many of their kids' piano recitals, soccer games, and school plays trying to manage the business of the church. They stop reading and growing intellectually, relying on old poetry that was hammered out long ago for another congregation. They no longer ask themselves on Saturday nights if they really believe this sermon they are about to preach. And one day, like Nouwen, they find that they are afraid to be alone with God for very long. That's the day the poetry becomes meaningless to them.

The congregation knows when something is amiss with their pastor. You don't have to be a poet to know when the authenticity of the verse is lacking. This creates anxiety for the congregation, which makes them focus more on the minor poet than on the poetry. A church can handle this for a while, but little of the church's mission will be accomplished until the focus gets off the pastor. It is for this reason that pastors have to be accountable to others, preferably a group of other pastors, who have the authority and the familiarity with their lives to catch them before they fall too far. There is nothing that pastors do for the congregation that is more important than taking care of their own souls.

So yes, I tell my students, pastors are role models for their congregation. But not models of perfection. What they model is confession, dependency, mystery, at times comedy, and always the pressing determination of the thirsty to find the stream that flows through their desert. In other words, they model the sufficiency of divine grace. That's the very thing that makes pastors intriguing.

CHAPTER 5

The Poetic Community

My stomach was complaining about the church's lasagna by the time I got to my car in the parking lot, and I really just wanted to go home. But I still hadn't seen Mr. Jefferson in the hospital. As I was pulling the car out of the driveway, I paused. Left for home, right to the hospital. I sighed and turned right.

It doesn't matter how many times I enter a hospital room — I will never get used to the sterility. There are no family photographs on the bedside table, no threadbare favorite chair in the corner, no smell of dinner wafting in from the kitchen. Instead there's a hospital bed with metal rails on the sides, whirling machines whose tentacles wrap around the patient, and smells that I don't want to recognize. No wonder people in here are sick.

Mr. Jefferson is an eighty-year-old African-American who retired ten years ago from a distinguished career as an appellate court justice. I had never called him by his first name, and he had never asked me to. Everyone, including his wife, called him Mr. Jefferson. But in spite of all this esteem, he was always kind and humble. He never accepted the many invitations to serve on one of the church boards, choosing instead to spend his extra time tutoring in one of the after-school programs we ran.

Since Mr. Jefferson had just come through a surgery that went longer than expected, the nurse had asked me to keep the visit short, and that certainly sounded good to me. But the patient had other ideas. I thought he was asleep, so my plan was to offer another quick prayer and then skedaddle. But as soon as I was in the room, he opened his eyes, smiled, and said, "I was just lying here praying for you." So now I felt terrible.

"How did it go today?"

"Well, you just missed the doctor. It seems they found the problem. Cancer — more than they could remove."

"Mr. Jefferson, I'm so sorry."

"And it's in the pancreas. Do you know what that means?"

"I know that's not good. What are they recommending?"

"They need to consult with the oncologists, of course, but I've never heard of anyone surviving this cancer. Have you?"

I paused and eventually came up with, "I'm not a doctor."

It was a punt. I had buried every one of my parishioners who was diagnosed with pancreatic cancer. Then it hit me. Mr. Jefferson had just been told that he had a terminal disease, and yet he was lying there praying for his pastor.

PASTORS ARE NOT THE ONLY poetic people in the congregation. In most congregations there are at least some people, strangely called the laity, who have long understood that there is a sacred subtext to the drama of their lives. They may be homemakers, lawyers, schoolteachers, or assembly-line workers, but that only describes how they earn a paycheck. Their true vocation is to live in communion with their Savior, or, as the Apostle Paul says repeatedly, to live in Christ. This is what we really mean by calling them Christ-ian. After a lifetime of hearing sermons, participating in home Bible studies, preparing Sunday school lessons, and attending conferences with titles like "The Laity at Work," they really did get the message — they have been yoked to Jesus Christ.

When Jesus Christ invited his disciples to wear his yoke, he was speaking to men from the countryside of Galilee who had seen a lot of animals pulling carts and plows. They knew that a yoke was used to bind two oxen together. Thus, to be yoked to Christ is to walk through all of life in union with him. Along the way the Holy Spirit binds believers deeper and deeper into the life of Christ until they begin to live his life. Even when he takes them to places they would rather not go, like a hospital, they learn to look for his sacred work of identity formation that is occurring just beneath the surface.

The laity may not always prefer theological language when it comes to describing their identity, but many of them do know what it means to live in Christ. If you asked them if they believe that the Holy Spirit has engrafted them into the Son's relationship with the Father, making them also the beloved, and if they believe that they have no higher calling than to find traces of the change in life that accompanies this adoption, they would say, "Well, yeah. Sure." The evidence of their belief is found in how they live their lives — quietly, faithfully, charitably, unafraid — just like their joint heir, Jesus Christ. But to be clear, they do not imitate the Savior's life; they participate in it.

The Poetry of Life in Christ

While it is popular to ask, "What would Jesus do?" the better question was always "What is Jesus doing?" The first question assumes that the Savior is on the sidelines and that the burden of life and work is on our shoulders. But in that case the Savior is not really saving but is setting impossibly high standards that we attempt to imitate by doing what we assume he would do *if* he were in our situation. On the other hand, the question "What is Jesus doing?" is built on the conviction that he is alive, reigning, and at work in our lives. In other words, he *is* in our situation, and that changes everything about our mission. Rather than believing that the work of Christ is completed and that now it is our turn to try to imitate his life and work, we take on the identity of being witnesses who watch and testify to his continued work of salvation that is unfolding before our eyes.

Clearly, Jesus' incarnation, ministry, cross, and resurrection make up the decisive turning point in the great drama of salvation. But the Kingdom is still coming. However, it comes not through our efforts at doing Christ's work, but through the ongoing ministry of the ascended and reigning Son of God, who completes his own work through the Holy Spirit. One of the means through which the Spirit fulfills Christ's work is by binding or yoking us to the life and work of the Son so that we may participate in what Jesus *is* doing.

By being yoked to Christ, we are able to follow him into the subtext of life, where he prefers to do most of his transforming work. Along the way, we not only learn how to discern the Savior's unapparent presence, but we also take on his character. It is similar to couples who have been happily married for over fifty years. They have spent so much of their lives bound together that they know each other's hidden ways, adopt each other's preferences, and eventually take on a common personality that has emerged out of their loving devotion. Sometimes they even start to look like each other. The longer we remain yoked to Christ, the more we take on his nature as children of God, and the more we realize that he has taken our humanity and restored it to the holiness for which it was created. Thus, when we speak of conversion, we are talking not about becoming a different person, but about becoming restored to the identity God gave us before our sin so corrupted life that we could no longer recognize ourselves. In Christ, we are made holy. This dynamic is traditionally referred to as sanctification, but it is never based on our success at imitating Christ. It exists only through our participation in the life of Jesus Christ, who is the only truly sanctified one.

This mystical union in Christ, as John Calvin referred to it, allows us to share in the gifts with which Christ has been endowed.[1] No gift is greater than the freedom to approach things like our own diseases as Christ does, not as things to be feared but as invitations to prayer. We pray not only for healing, but more importantly to receive more of the perfect love that casts out fear (1 John 4:18). And also like Christ, we soon find ourselves praying for others. Since we are yoked to him, we have no choice and eventually no inclination to do anything other than follow him into the other places in need of the Savior.

Only those who are unafraid can appreciate poetry, and sacred poetry always invites us beyond ourselves out into the expansive world where Christ is doing the most miraculous things.

It was not until my conversation with Mr. Jefferson in the hospital that I realized I had overlooked his true calling. I was in such awe of his former job that I had failed to see what he saw about his life's work of participating in Christ's mission on earth. Suddenly, his decisions about how he would spend his time in retirement made a lot of sense to me. All the stories I had heard about the uniqueness of his career and family life fell into place. And now I understood how he could receive such horrific news about his own health and calmly continue to work his way down a prayer list, as he always had.

---

1. John Calvin, *Institutes of the Christian Religion*, vol. 1, ed. John T. McNeill, trans. Ford Lewis Battles (Philadelphia: Westminster Press, 1960), 3.11.10, p. 737. For reference on the Holy Spirit's work of "engrafting" us into this mystical union, see 3.2.35.

This was not just a sick man lying in a hospital bed. I had been talking with someone made eternally alive in Christ — and he knew it. Mr. Jefferson's life was not going to be reduced by a pathology report any more than it had been amplified by a prestigious job description. Those were just texts. To help him discover his life, the Holy Spirit had led him down into the subtext, where he found the Spirit using any experience to bind him deeper into Jesus Christ's life. After a lifetime of training his eyes to see this holy mystery in all things, he could now be poetic, even with cancer.

Mr. Jefferson had found his poetry long ago, and he was determined to die as he had lived: by following the sacred sonnets of life. His life was but a mature expression of the ordination extended to all of us. But this is not to say that even the most saintly members of the church are poets. They are lovers of poetry, hopefully, but that doesn't mean they have to know how to write it any more than music lovers have to know how to play the violin.

The parish poet, by virtue of gifts, years of training, and a call to a particular congregation, is the pastor. This is the uniqueness of the ordination to Word and Sacrament. It has nothing to do with hierarchy and everything to do with the different apportionment of gifts. The cherished Reformation doctrine of the priesthood of all believers does not mean that we are all the same. It means that we are all called to fulfill our mission to live in Christ in the places where we have been called to serve him. The parish poet is nothing more — or less — than one of these priests who is called to expose the sacred subtext in the lives of all the other priests in the congregation.

There was a day when the pastor was perceived as an exalted and esteemed leader of the church and even the surrounding community. In most places that day has long since passed by, and rightly so. There is no ontological shift that occurs in the lives of those who kneel for the rite of ordination. They are still flawed human beings whose only claim to holiness is found in Christ, as it is for every other member of the church. But there is something different about the pastor, and, ironically, everyone in the pews is clearer about that than the person in the pulpit. This "something" has to do with the day that the pastor accepted the call to be their minor poet. Thomas Oden claims, "There remains a line as thin as a hair, but as hard as a diamond, between ordained ministry and the faithful layperson."[2] The thinness of the line is demonstrated by the pastor's need

2. Thomas C. Oden, *Pastoral Theology: Essentials of Ministry* (San Francisco: HarperSanFrancisco, 1983), p. 88.

for grace and by the faithful layperson's life in Christ. But the hardness of the line is found in the unique vow only the pastor takes to delve into the soul of the congregation in search of holy mysteries.

The Poetry of Witness

Every Wednesday morning I meet with a small group of men from my parish for Bible study. This group consists of doctors, lawyers, businessmen, and professors. When we gather, we discuss the intersections between the daily lectionary readings from the Bible and our lives. Over the years we have been a part of each other's diseases, divorces, jobs, weddings, marriages, and struggles with work and parenting. In spite of the seriousness of these issues, when the group started, most of the men would comment only on how wonderfully they were doing with life. This is what they had learned to do in all of the informal conversations they had had in their workplace. If they dared to confess the truth, it could and probably would be used against them. But in time they discovered that this group could be the much-yearned-for sanctuary where they were free to confess weakness and limitation.

Since we want to be more than a support group, every time we meet we struggle to find our lives in the major poetry of Holy Scripture. That's why I'm there. I would love to think that I'm just one of the guys around this circle, but none of the other men think that. They know that I'm there as their pastor. I still share my own personal issues and struggles, but I'm the only one around the circle with the additional calling to be a minor poet who pokes holes between the text and the subtext, "rightly handling the word of truth" (2 Tim. 2:15) that reveals God's involvement beneath the routines of all our lives. Everyone in the group knows what the Scriptures say. My place in the circle is to help them see what it means. As soon as I indicate the confessional relevance of a text, the discussion takes off at a speed so fast that I can barely keep up with it. Why? Because every man in the group is so excited to meet himself, his real self, his identity in Christ.

Of course, not all small groups within a congregation can or should have a pastor sitting in their circle. Often the presence of a pastor will only inhibit the exercise of lay leadership in the group, and so it is important that most small groups find their balance and rhythm without the clergy sitting at the table. My point here, however, is that when a pastor is present, she or he can never be deluded into thinking that the pastoral identity has been set aside. The pastor is always the pastor when surrounded by members of the congregation. This is even true in social settings, and certainly true when a small group of the church has gathered with the pastor around a table with their Bibles open.

After years and years of directing flashy church programs and speaking at more conferences than I can remember, I am convinced that sustained transformation of human lives occurs best through these small circles of Bible study that meet in living rooms, dorms, conference rooms, and coffee shops all over the world. Since these groups exist under the radar of pollsters, I have a strong hunch that they are more significant than is generally appreciated. What is actually occurring in each of these small groups is the creation of missionaries. These are not necessarily Bible-thumping evangelists who are crazed with passion to convert the world, but they are believers who are passionate about witnessing Jesus Christ's conversion of every corner of the earth, including the little corners where most of their lives are spent.

Witnesses don't really do very much. We have somehow twisted the term to make it more creative than Jesus intended it to be when he gave the Great Commission. Often when pastors call their congregations to witness, what they really mean is that it is the laity's responsibility to convert their neighbors and friends. But that is asking too much. Only Christ converts. When the risen and about-to-be-ascended Christ tells his disciples "You will be my witnesses," he implies that he will continue to be the creative force for salvation in the world and that his disciples are now sent out as apostles who witness this work that remains his alone. The witness merely sees and speaks about what he or she sees. Ask any courtroom judge, and you will be told that the last thing we need is for the witness to be creative.

This is not to say, however, that it is easy to witness the work of Christ. It takes a lot of time and hard work to learn how to recognize it. This is why people need pastor-poets. I have used the phrase "pay attention" so many times in my sermons that it now brings a gentle smile to most of those in the pews. They are getting used to following their preacher as I peel away the layers of the texts of boring or demanding jobs, health concerns, inevitable losses, family divisions, and fear about the volatility of the world — always in search of the subtext that reveals glimpses of Christ, who is making all things new. And when they come to church with their hearts full of excitement over the new baby, the wedding, the graduation, or the job they just received, they have to know how to give thanks to the Savior from whom all blessings flow. Without this witness, they will never be ready for the day they have to give these blessings back.

When Christians take on the vocation of being witnesses, it has a dramatic effect on how they conduct their lives. They stop trying to achieve a life and choose instead to receive one. As long as their goal was achievement, their constant companion was complaint because they could never achieve enough. But the day they decided to start witnessing the many ways God is still creating their lives, their companion became gratitude. Even when their lives take a hard turn, there is still opportunity for quiet moments of thankfulness, because by now they have learned how to find the manna and the gentle stream that flows into every desert.

I doubt that there is such a thing as a measure of spirituality, but if there is, gratitude would be it. Only the grateful are paying attention. They are grateful because they pay attention, and they pay attention because they are so grateful.

Poetry for Routines

Nothing makes us more grateful than having a clear sense of our mission in life. None of us can stand the idea that we are just taking up space on the planet. Our souls yearn to believe that we were created for a purpose, and we want to know what that purpose is. We want to know what we are called to do with life.

During the end of the Communist regime in Czechoslovakia, playwright Václav Havel was imprisoned for his stand against totalitarianism. After his release, he became the celebrated president of the free Czech Republic. During his four and a half years of confinement to hard labor, Havel wrote some powerful reflections on life under the guise of letters to his wife. These have been published as *Letters to Olga*. In these letters, Havel claims that he can withstand the great difficulties of prison if he can discover the meaning to life. The breakthrough in his struggle to make this discovery comes when he claims that the secret of human beings is the secret of their responsibility.

We may not be in prison, but we know about hard labor. We understand hard work on the job, at school, at home, and in the very hardest work of all — which is maintaining healthy relationships. When we get overwhelmed by our hard labor, the thing we most want to know is, Is this really my responsibility? Is this really what I'm supposed to do? Is this my calling? So isn't it fascinating that when the Apostle Paul is near the end of his life in Rome, and is writing one of his last letters to the churches — a letter that is all about calling — he begins this letter by writing not about our work, but about the work of God? It is as if he is saying that we will never understand our calling until we first understand the calling reserved for the Holy Spirit.

"I am confident of this," Paul writes after years and years of hard labor, "that the one who began a good work among you will bring it to completion by the day of Jesus Christ" (Phil. 1:6). The word in the Greek that is translated as "work" is *ergon*. It has the connotation of purposeful, productive activity. In physics an erg is a measurable unit of work. So what Paul is trying to say is that God's involvement in our lives is purposeful, concrete, and sometimes even measurable. Just as the Spirit of God once moved over creation, pushing aside the darkness and chaos, creating beauty and light in its place, so the Holy Spirit is now moving over our lives in specific, measurable ways.

When we look at our lives, this creativity may be hard to see. Our eyes can focus on the dark disease that lurks in our bodies, or on the chaos of a life that is not working out as we dreamed, or on the banality of a job that is going nowhere. But that is only because the creativity of the Spirit is not finished. As anyone knows who has watched an artist at work, the early stages of creation are hard to appreciate. The painter begins with strange lines and splashes of color that make no sense to the layperson. The sculptor appears to form only formlessness. Only the artist understands where the work is headed until the art is completed.

So if it is the calling of the Holy Spirit to continue the artistry of God in our lives, what then is our calling? For that we turn to Paul's conclusion in the letter to the Philippians: "Keep on doing the things that you have learned and received . . . , and the God of peace will be with you" (4:9). Keep on doing whatever is true, honorable, just, pure, pleasing, whatever is commendable, Paul concludes, and God will be with you. That's our mission — finding God with us in all of the ordinary places of life and being grateful for such extraordinary communion.

After wasting far too many years trying to do the spectacular, it has finally occurred to me that God loves routine. All of creation holds together by the same things happening again and again, whether those are great things, like planets revolving around stars, or very small things, like electrons going around and around their nucleus. And with each rotation, year after year, through winter, spring, summer, and fall, if you are paying attention, you can almost hear the doxology: "Praise God, from whom all blessings flow." Similarly, we are not asked to be other than a part of this created order who get up, go to work, care for children, make meals, do laundry, pay bills, and go to bed, only to rise the next morning to do it all again. "Keep on doing . . . ," the apostle commends. But along the way, those whose pastors have taught them to pay attention do it all as doxology.

There are so many reasons for gratitude scattered throughout the day. To begin with, the new day wasn't promised. I've buried enough parishioners who died in the night to make that clear. Neither is the grace of a job promised, and every church has plenty of people who are out of work to remind us of this. Children certainly are not guaranteed. And the health to get through the demanding schedules we keep is an extraordinary blessing. Who is most impressed with the amazing complexity of what it takes to keep a body healthy? Physicians are, because they understand it best. If a doctor is not impressed with the miracle of the human body, he or she is simply not paying attention. Just beneath the surface of the ordinary, the most amazing miracles can be found. But you have to knock on the door of the routine to have it open to you.

In response to Václav Havel, that's the secret of our responsibility.

Poetic Leadership

What would the world be like if it were run by sacred poets? That is exactly the question answered by the biblical notion of the Kingdom of God. It would be a world in which enemies are loved, the poor inherit the earth, and no one hurts another out of anxiety about what tomorrow may bring. These words depict the wisdom of heaven, but they appear foolish and naïve when spoken anywhere on earth. So the poet stands in the midst of a world that has grown jaded with reality and speaks in such a way as to open the doors into the Kingdom of Truth. The poet's lifelong apprenticeship is to move others, stir them from their sleepy reality, and awaken them to the presence of the Kingdom in their midst.

T. S. Eliot once complained that the characters of contemporary literature no longer have great ideals that either inspire or conflict them. Now characters only have nervous reactions. Great and almost epic ideals such as heroism, sacrifice, passion, and the pursuit of truth are hard to find in literature today because they are hard to find in the nervous and reactive society that our literature depicts. It's even hard now to find a thoughtful tragedy. That's because there is no room for either the pursuit of great ideals or the contemplation of our epic conflicts as long as the heart is anxious.

In a postmodern society, in which people are more aware of the failures than the promises of modernity, anxiety rules. Marriages now break apart as easily as the shiny appliances in our new kitchens. Jobs are lost in the volatility of corporate takeovers. Medicine can prolong existence, but not life. Soaring skyscrapers, a towering triumph of modernity, can tumble to the ground if a few crazed terrorists get their hands on a plane. And in spite of what it says over the mantles of many college doors, knowledge has made many wealthy, but it has not set us free. You don't have to be a sociologist to feel the contingency of life today. It's written on the faces of homemakers who walk the aisles of grocery stores worried about how they will keep their families together. Who has room to think about truth?

So it is not surprising that the pastors' continued devotion to great and holy ideals would put them out of step with the nervous reactors in a congregation. But that is part of what it means to lead them as poets. It's why we are there. Anyone can service anxious complaints, but it takes a parish poet to inspire and conflict a congregation with eternal truth.

The difference between the pastor as nervous reactor and the pastor as ideal-laden poet is marvelously illustrated in the contrast between Aaron's approach to leadership and Moses' approach to it. After only three months into their wilderness sojourn, the people became anxious because they thought Moses was gone too long on his journey up Mt. Sinai, where he was receiving a word from the Lord. This is not unlike the anxiety that a congregation always feels when they believe their pastor devotes so much time to reading, praying, and maintaining the spiritual disciplines necessary to finding poetry for the pulpit. So the people complained to Aaron: "Who will fix me? Who will take away the things that make me afraid?" Rather than seeing this complaint as a veiled longing for God, which is what all complaining is really about, Aaron attempted to make the complaint go away by giving the people what they wanted: a golden calf. To the Hebrews this was a more familiar and predictable image of a god. This god was fashioned by human hands, was not particularly mysterious or embarrassing, made incredibly attractive promises, and, best of all, placed absolutely no demands on the people. When Aaron heard the people's laments, he must have thought that he knew how to help Moses, and God, by taking care of the problem for them. So he gave the complainers what they wanted. He took their gold rings and fashioned them into a calf.

When the people saw his splendid work, they danced around it and sang, "These are your gods, O Israel, who brought you up out of the land of Egypt!" But Aaron said, "Tomorrow shall be a festival to the LORD" (Exod. 32:4-5). This means that while Aaron was thinking he had only given the people a symbol for worshiping the one God, the people themselves were treating the calf as their idol. There is a very thin line between symbols and idols. It takes a poet to know the difference. Churches are filled with symbols: crosses, liturgies, music, clergy, and even the building itself can appropriately symbolize our true worship of Yahweh. But the moment we "need" any one of them, they have lost their symbolic value and have become idols.

There is a tremendous amount of concern among pastors these days to make the Gospel relevant. Typically what they mean by this is that the church must do all that it can to address the felt needs of people as a way of attracting them to church. So worship services, musical offerings, and sermons are constructed in such a way as to scratch the itch of those in the pews. Programs are developed in the church to provide responses to human needs and are marketed in such a way as to make them superior to the products of the nonreligious competitors. The youth clearly need their own program, everyone assumes, but now so do the singles, the young married couples, the men and the women — and we dare not forget about the elderly, who have given so much to the church. Pastors knock themselves out not only to run this ever-growing enterprise but also to fulfill the insatiable needs of those who believe the church just isn't doing enough. The danger of all this relevance is that as soon as the church begins to respond to felt needs, it isn't too long before the pastor is making a golden calf. And as I have learned the hard way, it's a lot easier to make a golden calf than to get rid of one.

The alternative to being relevant is to be confessional. By this I refer not to the confession of sin, but to the church's historic practice of confessing faith in a particular context. This approach also takes felt needs seriously, but only as the presenting issue. To be confessional is to refuse to accept the agenda as it is self-described and to insist on interpreting all human needs from a biblical perspective. When the pastor does this, he or she reveals the underlying truth beneath the felt needs of the congregation. So rather than developing a "seven day a week" church that fills up the members' lives with church activity, the poetic pastor will wonder why these folks need the church to be a subculture that keeps them so busy with religious activity that they never have a chance to follow Christ out into the surrounding world. Rather than creating an attractive youth program that reassures parents that their kids will only hang around other Christians, the confessional church trains its teenagers to be witnessing missionaries in the various activities of their schools. Church programs are not inherently wrong, but the effort that begins with making the Gospel relevant to individual felt needs inevitably ends with the creation of idols. From the moment the Hebrews danced around their calf in the Sinai, it has always been the function of an idol to provide a substitute, humanly created savior for the frightened soul. And, like Aaron, the pastors who construct this idol will always say that they were just trying to help people worship the Lord. By contrast, the poetic pastor will insist on the historic confession that the church's ministry is not about making the Gospel relevant to the individual but about making the individual relevant to the Gospel. It's not about you. You are about it.

While he was on Mt. Sinai, Moses learned about the idolatry of the people from Yahweh. God was so furious that he told Moses, "*Your* people, whom *you* brought up out of the land of Egypt, have acted perversely. . . . Now let me alone, so that my wrath may burn hot against them and I may consume them; and of you I will make a great nation" (Exod. 32:7, 10, emphasis added). In other words, God was saying, "Moses, let's abandon this congregation to its destruction. I have a new church for you." Most pastors would have taken God up on this very attractive offer. But since Moses had spent enough time on Sinai to know the heart of God, he reminded him that these are "*your* people, whom *you* brought out of the land of Egypt with great power and with a mighty hand." Then, in one of the most amazing texts of the Bible, we are told that Moses changed God's mind "about the disaster that he planned to bring on his people" (Exod. 32:11-14, emphasis added). How do you do that? How do you change God's mind? Only poets can accomplish such an amazing feat.

Poets stand between the God and the people they have vowed to serve. They carry both in their souls. Sometimes they seek to plead the pathos, failures, desperation, and sins of the people to Yahweh, but without taking a breath they also proclaim the holy words of God to the people. This means that the pastor-poet lives with an agitated soul that is always filled with holy arguments between Yahweh and the people God loves but often finds difficult to love. The poet belongs to both Yahweh and the people.

When Moses confronted the people, he was severe in his words of judgment to them, but when he dared to confront God, it was only to hold up the covenantal claims to love, forgive, and carry the people even through their repeated faithlessness. Thus, the poet is more committed to the covenant between the people and God than to either the expressed needs of the people or the poet's own anger at their refusal to satisfy them.

Poets are devoted to the great ideas they have received from God above anything else, including their ideas for God. Moses didn't change God's mind by suggesting, "Well, sure, the people are idolaters, but they're not bad idolaters." The only hope for the people, Moses knew, was to remind God of the great and sacred idea called a covenant: "These are *your* people." This is the sacred poetry to which the pastor is committed. The place where this poetry resides is in the soul of the poet, a crucible in which holy words and profane anxiety get mixed together.

If our only allegiance is to the people, then we will always fall into Aaron's mistake of servicing complaints as one more nervous reactor. If our only allegiance is to God, then we will always seek our own redemption at the expense of the church we are serving. But the poet belongs neither to the people nor to the spirituality of the poet. The poet belongs to the sonnets of covenantal love between God and the frustrating people whom God cannot abandon.

PART II

The Craft of the Minor Poet

CHAPTER 6

The Subtext of Scripture

I could tell that Mr. Jefferson was tired and needed his rest. So I thought the time had come to excuse myself from his hospital room. But I knew that he would want his pastor to read some Scripture and pray with him.

First I prayed silently, asking for guidance in choosing the right text. Before I was done praying, I knew what to read.

"Therefore prepare your minds for action; discipline yourselves; set all your hope on the grace that Jesus Christ will bring you when he is revealed. . . . As he who called you is holy, be holy yourselves in all your conduct; for it is written, 'You shall be holy, for I am holy.'"[1]

He smiled when I got to the end. He knew what I knew about this text.

THIS MAY SEEM like an odd choice of Scripture to read to a man who was lying in a hospital bed with terminal cancer. How much "action" and "discipline" did he have left in him? Was it really necessary to call him to holiness at this time in his life? Yes, but not as a goal for which he had to strive. The call to holiness in this text is not an imperative. It's a promise. We *shall be* holy because Christ is holy. That was Mr. Jefferson's only hope, and he knew it. This man had spent most of his life discerning what it meant to live in union with Christ. By this time, at the end of his life, he

---

1. 1 Peter 1:13, 15-16.

would tolerate nothing less than a description of his true identity as a Christian.

There he was, lying before me with surgical tubes pouring drugs into him, and small wires pulling measurements of his heart out of him. His breathing was hard, and every word he insisted on speaking seemed to cost him. But I knew I was looking at holiness. It was never about Mr. Jefferson, and it was always about the holy grace into which he was baptized and had lived his life as a response. In my experience as a pastor, people don't make dramatic changes at the end of life. They die as they lived. And so it was important for me to affirm the great truth by which this saint had lived his life — to state on his behalf who he really was. It was his only comfort.

In order for me to read First Peter as a description of his life, however, it was critical that I as his minor poet knew how to look beneath the text to the subtext where I found his life. We've all heard too many sermons on this text that never did the hard work of peering beneath the words to discover the meaning. The slightest bit of exegetical effort reveals that the Greek doesn't require us to interpret the phrase *shall be* in the imperative. If it is seen as a promise, then the whole meaning changes dramatically. It is no longer an impossible standard for our work in spirituality, but becomes a reassuring blessing of the work of Christ in our lives.

It takes some time and a lot of practice to learn how to find the portals in Scripture that allow the pastor to serve as a minor poet. But the subtext is always waiting. As the late New Testament scholar Bruce Metzger used to tell us in seminary, "The text doesn't mean what it says. It means what it means." This chapter is devoted to methods of discovering the subtext, or what a text means for a pastor.

Exegesis for Poets

Any seminary, Bible college, or university religion department that takes biblical texts seriously teaches its students how to "rightly handle the word of truth" (2 Tim. 2:15). They all teach the importance of approaching a particular text in such a way as to insure that it is given its own voice. Thus, the message of the text is discerned through exegesis, which means reading it for its own meaning, which is pulled out of the words. The assumption of this technique is that the text's original meaning can be discerned by paying careful attention to such scholarly disciplines as defining the margins of the pericope, translating it from its original language, understanding the text in light of the larger literary framework, attending to the historical and theological framework of the author, and then discerning what the abiding words of truth may be.

The worst thing, we all learned in school, was *eisegesis*, which reads a particular meaning into the text. But in recent years, postmodern scholars have questioned our ability to ever approach an ancient text without some preconceptions that are culturally and even individually shaped. For example, a Third World pastor will inevitably find that the text has some different abiding words of truth than those found by the American pastor, regardless of how faithful they both are to exegetical methodology. Similarly, an inner-city African-American female pastor cannot set aside her identity in approaching the Scriptures any more than a suburban white male pastor can. This isn't necessarily eisegesis, but it does seem to support the whole notion that we can never fully appreciate the original intent of the biblical authors. When it comes to reading the Bible, we are inheritors of a particular tradition, and we have to be honest about the ways this cultural tradition has influenced our discernment of its truth.

Rather than struggle against this particular postmodern argument, which seems quite convincing, the contemporary pastor has the challenge of finding his or her culture not in the world of the text but in the world of the subtext. We honor the text as ancient and yet eternally sacred literature. That means we are still bound to follow all of the careful methods of good exegesis. Ironically, it is this exegetical technique that is so committed to honoring the original author's intent that opens the text to its subtext where the culturally conditioned yearnings and expectations are met. As a minor poet, the pastor has the calling first to honor the work of the major poets of the Bible. Only then can the Word of God be found for the unique people the pastor serves.

This is what we mean when we claim that the Holy Spirit inspired the Bible. It is the Word of God because it draws us to Jesus Christ, the Word made flesh. Any text can do that, revealing the Word for people as diverse as an Indonesian farmer and a New York attorney — if it is being rightly handled by a skilled minor poet who knows how to find a particular congregation just beneath the surface of the ancient text.

What pastors are always searching for is *kerygma*. That means we are looking for the point of contact between the text and the congregation. But this contact point has to be confessional, allowing the text to make its own claims to the particular issues and questions of a people. So we do not read the text through the lens of our church's culture, but we read the culture through the lens of the Scripture. This allows the text to confess or to speak kerygmatically into particular contexts. Thus, we are constantly building a confessional pathway that begins in the world of the Bible and ends in the congregation. When as pastor-poets we prepare the way of the Lord and build our kerygmatic confessions to our congregation, we find that we have ended up not in a different place than the Bible but in the subtext beneath it. That is the art of all minor poetry, which does not lead people away from the text, or what it says, but down into the eternal truth that reveals what it means for us.

There are many interpretive questions that the minor poet finds helpful in trying to find the kerygma. None of them have easy answers, but in asking them the pastor is launched into a hermeneutical adventure that usually ends with confessional discovery. This is critical in the preparation of sermons, but applicable to any pastoral effort at finding a biblical understanding of the congregation. Following are just some of the important exegetical questions to ask of the text.

What are the hard parts?

Whenever a pastor is preparing a sermon, the temptation is overwhelming to skip over the difficult and less-than-popular lines of a text. When Jesus tells an applicant for discipleship who only wanted to bury his dead father that we have to let the dead bury the dead, we are made uncomfortable by his severity (Luke 9:60). But a minor poet can never take on the role of being the public-relations official for Jesus. Not only is that not the minor poet's role, but it is also too easy. The challenge is to find the hopeful kerygma even in severity. Perhaps there really is no hope in focusing upon the dead. "How has our church been doing that?" the pastor wonders.

At other times the difficult part of a text is found simply in the flow of the narrative. For example, one morning when Peter was in a fishing boat, he saw his risen Lord on the shore. He then put on his clothes and jumped into the water (John 21:7). "Why would he do that?" the preacher asks early in the sermon preparation. Usually we take clothing off before jumping into water. Clearly, this piece of the story was important, or the Gospel-writer would not have included it. But why is it important? Of course, the question cannot be answered conclusively, but the minor poet still has to press it.

Our churches are filled with people who also want to dress up before approaching Jesus. "Why would we do that?" the preacher asks, allowing the rephrased question to hang in the air over the congregation.

How does translating help?

Anyone who has learned the original languages of the Bible has discovered how much color they add to the readings. Since the minor poet is dedicated to the calling of translating the work of the major poets to a particular people, it only makes sense that he or she has to know how to read the languages in which the sonnets were written. Most of us pastors slugged our way through Hebrew and Greek in seminary, but found it difficult to keep these language skills sharp after we took our final exams. But even if we are not still fluent in the tongues of Jews and Greeks, we can make use of the dusty reference books on our shelves to parse verbs in search of hidden meaning. It just takes time, like all poetry.

While preaching on the familiar text of Romans 12:1-2, I noticed that the phrase "be not conformed to the world" was written in the middle passive voice of the Greek. This means that it is something we do to ourselves. "Do not conform yourselves to the ways of our society," I said to my congregation. And then I was able to spell out some of the ways that we attempt to do this through our efforts at becoming a success by our own hard work, or by trying to self-construct a life through our choices, or simply by trying to collect as much as we possibly can. These are all agendas of our society that relentlessly confront us. "But be transformed," the apostle continues. And since that phrase is written in the passive voice, it calls us to a life of receiving the work of Christ. Most American congregations today are filled with people who do not know a thing about receiving. Had I not taken the time to work through the language in which Paul wrote, I would have missed this confessional proclamation to the over-achieving church I serve.

What stands out?

Often a passage of the Bible will have a line that seems odd if it is read with fresh eyes. Since pastors read these passages so often, their eyes have been trained to skip over these strange little phrases. But that is to miss an invitation to find a new place to mine the text. Minor poets so revere the work of the major poets that they assume there are no throwaway lines.

When Jesus was about to feed the five thousand, according to Mark, he ordered the people to sit down on the green grass. Why are we told that the grass was green? None of the other Gospel-writers includes this description of the lawn. Is it to say that all creation is blessed by the power of Christ? Or does it make a statement about the need simply to sit down and see the goodness of creation in order to pay attention to the miracles Jesus can offer? The response the pastor makes to this odd little addition that Mark makes about the grass will depend on how his or her congregation becomes blind to Christ.

At one point the Gospel-writer John claims that when the disciples dragged their full net to the shore, it contained 153 fish (John 21:11). That number seems very specific. This isn't the only time the disciples ended up with a full net of fish in the presence of Jesus, but it is unique to be told exactly how many fish were in the net. Why are we given this number? How could John have known this? Well, the congregations I've served are filled with people who could tell me the exact details of every success they've had in life. But salvation isn't about that. It's about the presence of Jesus with us, and so I never preach about fish. I just use the exact number as a means of depicting our own preoccupation with things that do not really matter. What matters is that Jesus is near.

～～～

What are the conflicts?

Like all good literature, the Bible frequently uses conflict to reveal a truth that is deeper than the issue that is being described. Sometimes this is obvious. When preachers approach a text that describes Jesus' conflict with the Pharisees, we never warn our congregations about the dangers of joining the ancient religious party known as the Pharisees. No, we always look beneath this particular conflict to warn about pretensions to self-righteousness. But we have to dig quite a bit deeper to discover that Pharisees were really good people who made great neighbors, always paid their bills on time, and were good, law-abiding citizens. At this point our congregations start to squirm a bit more. So rather than bashing the Pharisees as the only ones in conflict with Jesus, we will choose to depict Jesus' conflict with us.

Conflicts are even more interesting when they are found within an individual. When Peter was standing in the courtyard of the high priest being interrogated about his discipleship, his Lord was inside on trial. The way that the eighteenth chapter of John depicts this, the scene keeps shifting back and forth between the courtyard and the interior of the house. Inside, Jesus tells the high priest that his disciples will testify on his behalf. Then the scene shifts back outside, where we hear Peter deny Jesus three times: "I am not, I am not, I am not a disciple of Jesus." But a minor poet digs beneath these claims and begins to wonder if this is really a denial. Perhaps Peter is telling the truth for the first time. If being a disciple means following Jesus, then we have to wonder if Peter really qualifies. As he warmed himself by the fire, staring into the flames, he had to wonder this himself. For three years he had tried to prevent Jesus from doing exactly this. He was willing to do the most heroic things to help Jesus. But he could not follow him to the cross. "How about you?" the preacher asks as she begins to wrap up her Passion Sunday sermon. "Are you willing to give up being a hero for Jesus? Are you still a disciple when Jesus leads you this close to the cross?"

What obvious thing is new to you?

After preaching Advent sermons for over twenty-five years, I always approach the very familiar texts of the season with exhaustion. Every year I tell my wife that this congregation already knows everything I do about Mary, Joseph, and their baby. "If they would just give me one new character in the Nativity story, I could finish my ministry." But she knows how this goes, and she tells me just to return to the text. And every year I find something that I have never seen before. Like a dedicated dog, the minor poet just keeps gnawing on the bone until the kerygma appears.

The hard part isn't finding something new or clever in the text. What is difficult is finding the congregation in the same text over and over. Anyone can preach on obscure passages of the Bible. A minor poet earns his or her salary on the days that the congregation is certain they know everything there is to know about a text. But those in the pews will not be startled by the power of God's Word unless the preacher is. No one should be more surprised on Sunday morning than the person in the pulpit.

Often there is a phrase in a narrative that suddenly seems so obvious, but the pastor has repeatedly passed over it. Recently, when I was preaching from the second chapter of Mark, and not for the first time, I made one of these obvious discoveries. This is the passage that describes the faith of the four men who lowered their friend through the roof in order to place him in front of Jesus. But the text begins by telling us that Jesus was at home. I had never seen that before. Possibly this means that it was his home, or at least the house he was calling home, that was ripped apart by the men of faith. The narrative ends by Jesus telling the formerly paralyzed man to stand up, take up his mat, and go to *his* home. The image of home suddenly provided for me the interpretive bookends to the text. That allowed me to confess an abiding truth to a transient congregation: Until we find healing by being at home with Jesus, we'll never be free to find our own homes.

Every minor poet will, over time, develop favorite exegetical questions of the text. This list is not exhaustive but suggestive. The point is that the kerygma the pastor confesses to the congregation is going to be found not on the surface of the text, but underneath it. It is found only by a careful and at times relentless interview of the text.

Every week, I begin this process on Monday morning. And I spend the next few hours continuing to peel back the words of the text in search of the congregation's words. This search continues through the rest of the mornings of the week. The afternoon luncheons, appointments, visits, and counseling sessions provide a great deal of help. Even an evening committee meeting can help me understand the congregation's side of the sacred conversation that is occurring between the holy words I read in the morning and those of the people I love. By Thursday I'm usually wondering how this conversation will ever come together, because the text and the congregation seem to be talking past each other. I question why I chose to preach on this text and flirt with the idea of finding something easier for the sermon. But that's when the church secretary tells me that it's too late; the bulletin has already been printed. So I stick with the hard interview of both text and congregation. It is never until the end of the week that the breakthrough occurs. As Annie Dillard writes, "One line of a poem, the poet said — only one line, but thank God for that one line — drops from the ceiling."[2] I can write the rest of the sermon, but I've learned the hard way never to start until the line comes from heaven. That line is my path into kerygma.

Finding the Portals

Every text has a portal, a doorway that invites the minor poet to move from the text into the subtext. The interpretative questions listed above can provide assistance in finding these portals, but the structure and the narrative flow of the text will offer their own assistance.

The Gospels frequently begin a new pericope with the phrase "As they were going along the road . . ." (see, e.g., Luke 9:57). This is an often-repeated phrase in the Gospels that is used to introduce the most amazing events. It is as if to say that the Gospel always breaks into our lives when we thought we were just going along the road. After pointing this out, the preacher brings it home with a few lines that immediately follow: "You were just driving to work one morning when you saw a terrible accident. Then it occurred to you that the person in the accident was probably just driving to work as well. But suddenly everything turned upside down . . ."

When the pastor is working with one of the Epistles of the New Testament, the grammatical structure of the text offers a tremendous amount of exegetical help. This is particularly true for the writings of Paul, who took the structure of his arguments very seriously. This is seen in the first ten verses of the second chapter in Ephesians. In the first verse Paul begins with three startling words — "You were dead" — and then continues to describe the desperate conditions of our lives. In verse four, the argument dramatically turns with the phrase "But God . . . ," and then the apostle continues by describing our new and risen life in Christ. A brief passage that begins with us dead ends with us seated in "the heavenly places" (v. 6). And the turning point is "But God." All that the preacher needs to do in order to enter into the subtext where the congregation can be found is to

2. Annie Dillard, *The Writing Life* (New York: Harper Perennial, 1990), p. 75.

ponder the singularity of this phrase. "We cannot say," the preacher adds, "'I was in desperate trouble, but then I got a new job,' or 'but then I got married,' or 'but then I inherited a ton of money, and now I have found my way to the heavenly places.'"

When the minor poet approaches a narrative text, these portals into kerygma become almost irresistible. It doesn't matter whether the story comes from the Old Testament, the Gospels, or the book of Acts — every story is written in such a way as to invite readers to discover that this is not only an ancient story but the high drama of God's involvement in our lives as well. Below is an example of how to find the portals in the story of Jesus' encounter with the Samaritan woman at the well.

The Portal of a Twist: John 4:1-6

A narrative twist is a strange turn of events in the story. The characters aren't doing what we expect them to do, and thus the drama surprises us. The reason this is a portal is that it opens up a means of discovering the startling nature of the Gospel in all of our lives.

The story in chapter four of John's Gospel begins by telling us that the Pharisees have heard that "Jesus is making and baptizing more disciples than John." In response to this great success, Jesus decides to get out of town. Most pastors don't decide to leave their current ministry because it has been too successful. Why would Jesus do so? It is then just a small step to wonder if we disciples of Jesus have the right understanding of success today.

Next we are told that "he had to go through Samaria" (v. 4) in order to return from Jerusalem to Galilee. But devout Jews never went through Samaria for fear of contaminating themselves with the sins of the Samaritans. Instead, they always went around this area that was in their way. What does it mean, then, that Jesus "had to" enter Samaria? Is this a statement about the Incarnation, which is a foundational theme for John? Or is it a prophetic statement about Jesus' insistence on taking the exit ramps off of the city bypasses that we prefer to ignore because they lead into the bad neighborhoods that are in our way?

This paragraph ends with Jesus taking a break from his journey by sitting at a well in the Samaritan town of Sychar. But the twist in expectation comes when the story tells us that he took the break because he was tired. Can Jesus, the Son of God, get tired? Of course he can if he is fully human. But since many Christians have a deficient Christology that depicts Jesus as essentially an ancient Superman, this news of his fatigue could be startling. What is the good news for us in having a Savior who knows what it means to get tired out by our journeys through life? First, it means he understands. But, more powerfully, it also means that our Savior takes on our deep weariness.

The Portal of Identification: John 4:7-18

When parishioners discover that this is not simply an old story about people long dead, but it is their story, then the Word of God is speaking directly. Most preachers know this and are always trying to build bridges between biblical characters' lives and our own lives. But the real challenge is not to point out similarities but to tell our contemporary life stories through the details of the biblical narrative. This is easier with some passages than with others, but it is always possible.

When Jesus and the Samaritan woman get into a discussion about water, the conversation doesn't seem to be going well. He keeps speaking about drinking from the living water. And he promises that whoever takes this water will never thirst again. But she is missing this metaphor, thinking that he's promising to "fix" her thirst so she never has to come back to the well again. When the contemporary congregation hears this familiar text read again, they are all tempted to roll their eyes and say, "She just didn't get it. He isn't talking about her physical thirst." Right. We know that Jesus is promising to quench the insatiable thirst of her soul. And we claim to have tasted this living water. So why then are Christians still so thirsty? Everyone in the church listening to this sermon is thirsting for something more in relationships, in work, in health, and most of all in spirituality. As soon as the sermon points to this identification with the woman, the pastor is no longer preaching about her but to us.

It is striking that we are not even given the name of this woman. She will always be remembered simply as the woman at the well. It's as if her desperate thirst has taken over her identity. That's the way our thirst works too.

Just to illustrate the depths of her thirst, Jesus points out to the woman that she has had five husbands and isn't married to the man with whom she currently lives. The commentators have a field day with interpretations of this woman's five husbands. The traditional interpretation is that this woman simply isn't good at marriage. But recently some feminist New Testament scholars have pointed out that in this time women didn't choose to whom they would be married. Given the Levirate marriage system, which was practiced by the Samaritans, this woman may have simply outlived the men who had to marry her after her first husband died. The sixth kinsman could have been afraid for his life if he made her respectable again. Maybe, but it doesn't really matter. The point is that no woman plans on being married five times. The system isn't working for her.

For the minor poet, the more profound point is that this woman depicts the depths of our own desperation. It would be easy for those listening to the sermon to let themselves off the hook by claiming that at least they haven't been married five times. Perhaps not. But they have tried five weight-reduction plans, five moves, five jobs, five degree programs, or five churches — and the system isn't working for them either. Now the preacher is beneath the text.

Once the minor poet learns to look for such portals of identification, they aren't difficult to find. And they always open up the text by allowing us to make proclamation into our own lives. Here's another example. When Doubting Thomas is presented in the Gospels, it is always as "Thomas the Twin." But we don't know a thing about this twin. It could be anyone. And there's the portal. "It could be you, couldn't it?" the preacher asks. "You decided to follow Jesus, but you've got your doubts too, don't you? Sure you do. I'll bet you could be Thomas's identical twin."

The Portal of a Disconnect: John 4:19-27

Sometimes the reader of a narrative is jarred by the absence of good flow in the text. It feels as if the train has come off the tracks because they weren't aligned. That's not because the story is badly written. The disconnect is given as a means of allowing us to get off the narrative track and into the truth of our own disconnections with the Gospel.

When Jesus invites the Samaritan woman to confront the truth of her painful history with relationships, and the even deeper truth of her thirsty soul, she abruptly changes the subject. Suddenly she starts talking about the old worship debates between the Samaritans and the Jews and asks Jesus if he has an opinion on this issue. It makes the minor poet wonder if our own contemporary worship debates serve the same function. Are we simply trying to distract both Jesus and ourselves with this old debate? Then one starts to wonder how many other bad questions we have for Jesus, and do they all serve the function of helping us remain disconnected from the questions he is asking us?

Jesus stays with this woman's distraction and makes a response about how his father desires to be worshiped — in spirit and in truth. It is essentially a Trinitarian statement. God is spirit, we are told. And by the end of the paragraph, Jesus identifies himself as the Messiah who brings the truth. This provides some of the most profound biblical theology we have for worship. But another disconnect comes in verse twenty-seven, when Jesus' disciples show up and are amazed not by his teaching but by the fact that he is speaking with a woman. Again, we see those who are supposed to be the experts on Jesus distracted by the wrong issue. Why? Because we would rather nurture our old arguments than worship.

The Portal of Irony: John 4:27-42

Irony is similar to a twist portal, but it turns our expectations in on themselves, depicting an outcome that is the exact opposite of what we expect. The reason that this is such a helpful portal to the minor poet is that it provides a wide-open doorway for discovering our inability to control spirituality. Trying so hard to become spiritual, we become Pharisees, which is ironic, since Jesus consistently denounced them for their lack of spirituality. And according to the Beatitudes, it is only the poor in spirit who inherit the kingdom of heaven. Again, once a minor poet gets a taste for irony, he or she finds it throughout the Bible.

While the disciples continue to fret over discovering their Lord talking with a woman, and then begin to worry that Jesus isn't eating well, the woman heads back to her town to tell people that she just may have found the Messiah. Isn't it ironic that the disciples, who are supposed to be evangelists, are preoccupied with non-issues, while the woman they were worried about goes home to do some evangelizing? "And wouldn't it be ironic," the preacher wonders out loud from the pulpit, "if the people we are most worried about are fulfilling our mission better than we are?"

This woman has been disgraced by her community, which is why she had to go to the well alone in the heat of the day. Even Samaritans have their standards. To be dis-graced means to be removed from the means of finding the grace of God. In ancient society, one's community was a necessary means of grace, and no one could be at home with God for long on their own. But the irony is that it is this woman, relegated to the margins of her community, who encounters Jesus, the one whom the Gospel of John presents as the means of grace for the whole world. So who is really disgraced — the outcast, or the respectable people? This woman brings people from the town of Sychar out to meet Jesus, and they then invite him into their community. The ironies are heightened by the end of this text, when the Samaritans claim that Jesus "is truly the Savior of the world" (v. 42), which is the first time, according to John, that anyone makes this declaration of faith about him. And who does that? The marginalized Samaritans.

After pointing to all of this irony in the text, the preacher cannot resist taking the precarious step of asking if Jesus isn't more likely to be found on the margins of our own community.

These are not the only portals that are written into the biblical texts. And the point is not to list or categorize all of them, but simply to train the eye to appreciate the text's own help in finding the kerygmatic truth that the minor poet is called to confess to a congregation.

Carefully making our way into these portals doesn't dishonor or manipulate the inspired nature of the text. To the contrary, exegesis of the subtext honors the holy nature of these texts, which are pregnant with the Word of Life. The minor poet is simply the midwife who serves the Holy Spirit in doing what only God can do — bring a congregation to life through the Word.

CHAPTER 7

The Subtext of Human Life

As I walked back to the hospital parking lot, I absentmindedly pulled out my cell phone to check for messages. The phone number of the missed call that flashed up on the screen was familiar. It belonged to Sally McGrath. She's the woman whose worship announcement I had affirmed earlier in the evening at the church.

I knew why she was calling. It was the same reason Sally always called. She was addicted to compliments, and I hadn't given her enough of them.

Sally is a sixty-something-year-old widow who still lives in the big house where she and her husband, Max, raised their children before he died from a heart attack four years ago. One of her sons now lives on the West Coast, and the other one is in London. She is generally gracious and kind with people, but she often appears harried.

Even before Max died, Sally had become a habitual church volunteer — the kind who signs up for more commitments than she can possibly complete and then complains about being overworked. I used to try to get her off the hook and tell her that we would find someone to take over her responsibilities. But I soon discovered that wasn't what she wanted. She was looking for affirmation, not of her work, but of herself. The only way she knew how to find it, though, was to look like she was killing herself for the church. Sally needs a twelve-step program for volunteering.

As I stared at my phone, I smiled and shook my head. Then I leaned against the fender of my car, dialed her number, and waited for the inevitable.

"Craig, you were so kind at the church dinner tonight, but I have to tell you that I really don't think I did a very good job with that announcement. And if we don't get more volunteers for Vacation Bible School, we're just going to have to cancel it this year. I'm thinking that maybe you should find someone else to direct this program. I'm not doing a very good job."

That was my cue to tell her that she was doing a wonderful job and that we would have a wonderful VBS under her wonderful leadership. She wanted to hear me say, "We can't make it without you." But I couldn't say that and fulfill my calling to be her pastor. So instead I said, "Sally, you're a wonderful woman. Why don't you stop by the church tomorrow so we can talk a bit?"

I HAVE KNOWN Sally McGrath for a long time — long enough to know all about her addictions. And I love her enough to refuse to keep feeding her the narcotic that will only continue to whittle away at her soul. The time had come to have a long and probably difficult conversation with her about her compulsive drive to find from her work what only God can give her. I knew it was quite likely that I would need to make a referral to a trusted therapist who could help her dismantle some of the psychological blocks that were making it impossible for her to hear the Gospel I presented from her pulpit. And I knew that my calling was not to be that therapist.

When a minor poet is attempting to discern the subtext of a parishioner, the agenda is not to find portals into the psyche. Pastors approach people differently than we approach the Bible. We have been trained to plunge into the biblical subtext by making our way through its portals. But in a human life these portals are actually complex mazes, which may lead to a violation of boundaries and will certainly lead the pastor onto a slippery slope that ultimately falls into therapeutic psychology. Parish poets avoid psychodynamics not because it is antithetical to the Gospel, any more than medicine is, but because we respect the limits of our craft. Every pastor keeps the phone numbers of good therapists close at hand, alongside the numbers of attorneys and doctors, in order to make referrals when this attention is required. We respect their years of training and finely tuned skills and refuse to become imposters of their trade.

The agenda for the minor poet is to read the parishioner biblically. That is what pastors are trained to do, and we're usually the only person in someone's life who has these skills. Why would we dispense what for us could only be pop psychology when we could be experts at the theological truth of human life? As minor poets, our ultimate loyalty is to the insights gleaned from the major poets. But we are also deeply loyal to our parishioners — enough to want to give them the best we can offer, which are the biblical words of life.

Even if I succeeded in getting Sally to see a therapist, I couldn't abandon her to those capable hands. I'm her only pastor. So I would invite her to keep seeing me even after her therapy began, not so that I could dabble in a little Christianized therapy, but so that I could keep doing what I know how to do — provide a theological interpretation of her life.

The Pastoral-Therapeutic Partnership

Occasionally the pastor runs into a situation where the psychological issues are more dramatic than the need to work on self-esteem. One Monday I received a phone call from a relatively new member, Jean Davis, who had heard my sermon the previous day on the text "I believe; help my unbelief" (Mark 9:24). Somewhere in the sermon I made the innocuous comment that both a believer and an unbeliever live in each of us. Jean asked me if she could come, soon, to talk about that phrase. It wasn't innocuous to her. When she arrived at my study the next day, she plopped down in the chair, breathed deeply several times, and then warned me that this meeting could "wig me out." She certainly had my attention.

Jean told me that she had struggled for most of her life with multiple personality disorder (MPD). After explaining some of the havoc this had caused in her life — failed relationships, jobs from which she had been fired for inappropriate behavior she couldn't remember, checks missing from her checkbook that were written by one of the other personalities — she then got to the question that was deeply troubling her. "What if I die in an altered state? What if the unbeliever in me is not baptized? Will I go to hell?" Her earlier warning was almost right. I wasn't exactly wigged out, but I was almost in tears as I pondered the pathos of her life.

Jean had not seen her therapist in a long time, and I knew she needed to get back into this difficult journey if she had any hope of bringing all of her personalities back home into the same life. But as a person who was spiritually motivated, she also wanted to know what God made of her fractured life. So I promised to keep seeing her, but only if she returned to her psychiatrist, and only if he and I could discuss my involvement in her ongoing therapy. She agreed quickly to these conditions, and a couple of days later I received a phone call from her doctor.

The psychiatrist thanked me for encouraging Jean to return to her work with him, and asked me about the sermon that had been so disturbing to her. By the end of the conversation, he had explained the dynamics of MPD to me and detailed the types of early childhood trauma and abuse that create this condition. He cautioned me to expect some of the "altered personalities" to appear on occasion in my meetings with Jean, told me how to handle it when this happened, and made it very clear that our goal was to seek the integration of these personalities within her. Then he said, "We need your help. I'll do the clinical work with her, but she needs her pastor to make it clear that she doesn't have to break apart her personality in order to find one that God will like." And so we began our work, psychiatrist and pastor, each fulfilling our callings by using our collected skills to help this tortured soul.

It took a long time — years, actually — but eventually Jean showed signs of integrating. The altered personalities gradually disappeared from my office and stopped writing me letters. And Jean was able to reconstruct a healthy life. The psychiatrist played a critical role in confronting the sexual abuse she had experienced at the hands of her mother. He helped her truly believe that she was not responsible for that and didn't need to disassociate from a "bad girl," who was actually a victimized good girl. My job was just to keep telling her that the arms of Christ on the cross were open wide enough to embrace everything and everyone within her. In my last meeting with her, Jean just kept saying, "In Christ all things hold together." It will always be the anthem of her life.

At no time did I take over for the trained therapist with a few ideas of my own about a psychological disorder as complex as multiple personalities. I didn't even share the burden of integrating her personalities, which was the job of the psychiatrist, Jean, and the Holy Spirit. My job was to be the pastor who believed for her that the Spirit was in fact with her, all of her. While that mission was simple, it was still critical, and I dared not abandon her to the therapist. Only a pastor can be the minor poet who speaks the biblical words of hope into a fractured soul.

Most of the care that pastors offer is not given to people whose issues are as extreme as Jean's were. More often we're dealing with the Sally Mc-Graths, who struggle with problems like never feeling that they're good enough. But the extreme illustration makes the point clear: the pastor can assist in the restoration of souls only by being the pastor and not by pretending to be a therapist. Pastoral pseudo-therapy is not valuable just because it's free.

Biblical Claims about Life's Subtext

The major poetry of the biblical-theological tradition makes eternal claims about all human life, claims that are as true today as they were when their ancient authors first penned them. But as is the nature of truth, it is not always evident, and typically it lies beneath the self-constructed veneer of life. For some this is a veneer of neatly ordered propriety. Others appear angry, driven, lonely, lost, shamed — and the list goes on and on. But the pastor refuses to accept these false presentations even whey they are accepted by the people who wear them. Instead, as a minor poet the pastor insists on interpreting all lives through the lens of the major poets, who reveal the truth that lies beneath the veneer.

When the pastor begins to describe this subtext, a flash of recognition should occur within the parishioners. For some it will feel as if the pastor is uncovering once-cherished treasure that has been buried beneath years of busyness and anxiety. This treasure may even be the soul itself. When this happens, some parishioners may sit back, gently smile, and think, "Yes, that's the part of me that I've been missing." Others will not respond so well to having their souls exposed, even to themselves. But even the vehemence of a refusal to entertain the biblical perspective indicates that the pastor has hit a nerve. Whether the major poetry is embraced or adamantly rejected is not the business of the pastor; it's the business of the Holy Spirit. We don't try to convince. The poet just speaks the poetry.

While the Christian theological tradition makes many truth claims about human life, it is possible to summarize those that a parish poet will most frequently encounter. This is not an exhaustive list, but a suggestive one. The human subtext has always been a topic of great concern to the major poets, and they wrote extensively on it. Although it isn't possible to provide an exegesis of all their claims, the following list demonstrates how to find a parishioner's subtext using theology rather than therapy.

Humans are made in the image of God.

Pastors never trust the self-image of anyone. That's because most people construct their identities from an assortment of borrowed images. The typical American today strives to be as attractive as the models on fashion magazine covers, as successful in work as Bill Gates, as sensitive a spouse and parent as Ward and June Cleaver, and as death-defyingly healthy as Lance Armstrong — all while maintaining the inner peace of the Dalai Lama. The fact that these images are often in conflict with each other creates tension within the heart of the individual, who tries desperately to meet all of their demands.

Typically the pastor is the only influence holding to the belief that life is a holy creation that can be rightly known only in the light of the image of God. As the old confession of faith states, our "chief end is to glorify God and enjoy him forever."[1] We were marked by God, for God, and the holiness of this image goes to the heart of our identity and mission in life.

The work of Jesus Christ in our lives is to restore this divine image, which has become so distorted that it can no longer be recognized. The distortion came about by our attempts to cram other images into our souls, which made it impossible for us to remember who we were created to be. The judgment for this sin is not only that it separates us from our Creator, but also that we are never able to satisfactorily construct the false images we envisioned. So we are always the not-good-enough spouse, parent, or worker, and the image of our bodies is never quite what we hope for. The judgments for losing this holiness show up every time we look in the mirror.

The restoration of Christ, often referred to as conversion, does not make us into different people but converts us back to what God designed us to be from the beginning — specifically, creatures who bear the mark of

---

1. See "The Shorter Catechism of the Westminster Confession of Faith," in *The Book of Confessions* (Louisville, Ky.: Office of the General Assembly of the Presbyterian Church, 1983), 7.001.

holiness. This is a progressive process through which we are changed "from one degree of glory to another" (2 Cor. 3:18). But our movement through this sanctification occurs not through our own efforts at developing piety. It is only as the Holy Spirit binds us into the life of Christ that we are able to take on his holiness. Thus, our spirituality is always vicarious, since it is through this union in Christ that we are made holy. He is the image of God that we bear on our lives.

The significance of this for pastoral encounters is found in the unique way we invite people to make changes in their lives. We do not peddle images of the super-Christian and tell our parishioners to try harder to attain this goal. That's just another false image. And it will also leave us only with more judgment by tossing the not-good-enough Christian onto our heap of failures. The only way out of the judgment trap is for pastors to keep pointing to the true image of the God in whom "we live and move and have our being" (Acts 17:28). This is the God revealed in Jesus Christ, "and we have seen his glory, the glory as of a father's only son, full of grace and truth" (John 1:14). So, with poetic irony, pastors help people to change not by talking about them, but by talking about the God revealed in Christ. As an irritated woman once said to me at the door following worship, "Jesus, Jesus, Jesus. Is that all you know?" Had I been thinking clearly at the time, I would have said, "It's all I know that can be of help to you."

Just because people call themselves Christian and have a long history in the church doesn't mean that they have a biblical image of God. To the contrary. The longer they've hung around religion, the greater the chance that they've acquired some false ideas about God that have a negative impact on their self-image. In pastoral counseling, the minor poet is constantly wading through these false images, which are the real blocks to their ability to make changes. We are made in the image of even a false god, and until the image of God is seen correctly in the grace and truth of Jesus Christ, we will never be able to gain a correct image of ourselves. When people tell me about their struggles with anger, a little digging reveals that they believe God is angry with them. Those who struggle with compulsive work patterns have been worshiping a demanding God who is never satisfied. People who have a hard time trusting their hearts to others don't really believe in the steadfast love of God. None of them can discover real change in their lives apart from a Christological view of God. So conversations that begin with improvements they want to make in life should end with the pastor demonstrating the changes Christ has already made to their lives.

Rather than using the few reflective listening skills we learned in our Introduction to Pastoral Care seminary classes, which is only another way of holding up the judgmental mirror, we pastors need to hold up Jesus Christ. "See him?" we say. "That's who you really are. Everything else about you is just pretending." Saying anything else would not be truly kind. The dangerous mythology of the day is that we are being loving when we accept people's self-understanding. But if that understanding is actually a false image constructed by the idols of contemporary culture, then the kind and loving gift is to unmask these lies about identity. The human self is never more truly itself than when it is living in Christ, the restorer of the holy image of God in humans.

This means that pastors always deflect excuses for pretending. I've lost count of the number of times that I've heard parishioners say, "I'm sorry I got into an argument at the committee meeting last night, but I have a short temper. That's just the way I am." I always reply, "No, it's not. You are who God made you to be, and God didn't make you angry. 'For we are what he has made us, created in Christ Jesus for good works, which God prepared beforehand to be our way of life'" (Eph. 2:10). Who would want to settle for less?

Human life is limited.

The first two chapters of the Bible provide our only picture of the life that God desired for us creatures. It was paradise. But we were not created to enjoy all of it. Planted in the middle of the garden was a tree whose fruit was forbidden. It is significant that this tree was not located off on the margins of Eden, where it could be ignored. Every day Adam and Eve had to walk past this reminder that they were not created to have it all. That is God's idea of paradise for us.

We all have something in the midst of our lives that is beyond our created reach. This is something we cannot freely take, something that reminds us that we are not gods who have it all. It may be a dream that will never be fulfilled, a desired relationship that remains only a desire, or a thorn in the flesh that's never removed. What the forbidden tree represents in a person's life is not as important as the realization that we humans were not created with the capacity to take whatever we desire. There can be 999 trees in our garden to which we can freely go and enjoy their fruit, but where do we pitch our tent? Under the one tree we cannot have. We begin to obsess over this thing that we do not have, and we let the rest of the garden go to weeds. How can we get the one thing that is missing? It's right there. So judging the garden that God gave us and called "good" to be not good enough, we reach for more than we were created to have.

As the story goes, it is then that we lose the garden, and it is then that we realize it was paradise. Only now it is paradise lost. As every pastor knows, the greatest regrets people have are not over their victimizations but over the things they've done to themselves.

From the beginning we have been created to be receivers, not achievers. Nothing is more countercultural to contemporary Americans. We have been raised to set our goals high, work hard, and achieve our dreams. Clearly there is merit to this work ethic, but it has limits, and the greatest one is that it seduces us into thinking that we are the creators of our own destinies. The only destiny that comes from reaching for whatever we want is finding ourselves east of Eden. Every page of the Bible presents God as the achiever and us as the receivers of this sacred, good work.

At no time is this more obvious to pastors than at Christmas, when our parishioners are knocking themselves out to achieve the perfect experience for their loved ones. It is amazing that the mythology of this dream is able to resurface every December in spite of its repeated failures. When I hear the aspirations that people have for their reuniting families, gathered around the piano wearing matching sweaters, joyfully singing carols, I always want to ask, "Is this the same family you had last year?" But no one is interested in reality checks at Christmas. So they knock themselves out to achieve what cannot happen. According the Nativity narratives, God is the only one who is giving at Christmas. The rest of us are doing all we can only to receive the gift of salvation. The only members of my parish who seem to understand this are the children. In all of my years of pastoral ministry, I have never had a child come to see me to talk about the stress of the holidays. They aren't worried about making it to all the parties, buying the perfect presents, maxing out their credit cards, and travel plans. As every child knows, the only stress of Christmas is how can we possibly wait for it to arrive — the day we receive so much.

As receivers we are inherently limited. We can hold only what is given to us, but this is a mercy, because it forces us to honor these gifts as blessings from God. Even the Law is presented as a grace in both the Old and the New Testaments because it provides limits within which we must live.

All of life is conducted within boundaries. Relationships have the limits of not being able to meet all of our emotional needs. Work cannot be a source of identity. Health and beauty cannot become idols. And to cross these limits is to discover that we have lost our ability to enjoy them as good gifts. Freedom is found not in escaping limits, but in discovering the goodness of life within them. Our culture tells us just the opposite. It claims that we won't be free until we buy the more expensive car or house, make the next move, or get the next promotion. But none of those achievements are capable of making us free. Typically, they only enslave us.

The subtext to human limits, which it takes a minor poet to see, is that these limitations are the very mark of our freedom. They create the opportunity to obey God and to humbly receive life with a grateful heart, even though something is missing. That is why the forbidden tree in the midst of the garden is so important to us. It is the means by which God has distinguished humans from the rest of creation with dignity. We alone have the capacity to choose to receive the life we have been given or to rebel in the futile effort to make a living on our own.

It takes a poet to help people find the ways in which God's ongoing creativity unfolds for them as a gracious gift. Life began as a grace. It is sustained every day with breath by grace, and one day it will enter eternity *sola gratia*. Along the way, all of the important blessings of life, such as relationships, children, opportunities, calling, and health have come to us not through our achievements but by the grace of God. No mission in life is greater than learning how to receive such overwhelming grace.

Frequently I will end a service of worship in our congregation by saying something like, "Every day this week you have to decide if you want to achieve your life or receive it. If you make achieving your goal, your constant companion will be complaint, because you will never achieve enough. If you make receiving the goal, your constant companion will be gratitude for all that God is achieving in your life." I'm not certain that there are such things as measures of our spirituality, but if there are, then gratitude is probably the best one. It indicates that we are paying attention.

As a minor poet, the pastor doesn't simply tell people to be satisfied with their limited lives but instead helps them to find the joy and sacred purposes to these limits. Some of the things that are missing from the garden are good and certainly desired. When a couple discovers that they cannot have children, when a spouse is buried, or when a terminal disease is discovered, it isn't helpful for the pastor to point to all of the other blessings in a person's life. What is helpful is for the pastor to walk into the sorrow in search of the sufficient grace of God. Anyone who finds more of the steadfast love of God from which we are never separated has found something far greater than that which is missing from the garden. And it is for that grace that we are most grateful.

Humans are the beloved of God.

When the Son of God insisted on being baptized by John, he was identifying himself as also being the Son of Man. John offered baptism for the remission of sins, a futile effort at washing away sins to make oneself righteous. According to Luke, even John was frustrated with the crowd who came to be baptized but did not repent or change their way of life (Luke 3:7). But as every pastor who carefully watches his or her parishioners knows, it isn't that people don't want to make changes to live righteously. They're simply too addicted to the sin that separates them from God. So the crowds in our church often do exactly what the crowd at the Jordan did. They come to worship, pray the printed confessions of sin, and hope that this liturgical act will wash away their sins. They also have other programs for self-improvement, such as trying a new diet, cutting down on drinking and smoking, or finding someone who will love them just right. But these things are all futile for making real change in our lives. This is why the old Pietists claimed that we are lost. And it is why John was amazed that the Lamb of God who takes away the sins of the world would insist on being baptized. But this is exactly what the Incarnation required of Jesus. He had to take on the futility of the human condition as the Son of Man. If he were to walk into our lives today, he could just as well arrive at our job interviews, wedding receptions, or retirement parties — the next futile thing we are trying to make life right.

John the Baptist was certain that when the Son of God arrived, he would bring a winnowing fork to separate the chaff from the wheat and throw it into unquenchable fire (Luke 3:17). But there is no salvation in such judgment. Salvation comes through a loving Savior who finds us and takes on our lost condition. As the poetry claims, "For our sake he made him to be sin who knew no sin, so that in him we might become the righteousness of God" (2 Cor. 5:21).

When Jesus came up out of the waters, the Holy Spirit descended upon him in the form of a dove. This is the same Spirit who came upon Mary to conceive the Incarnation, and who will drive Jesus out into the wilderness after his baptism to be tempted as all humans are. Day after day in Jesus' life, the Spirit was driving the Incarnation deeper and deeper. As the water of the Jordan was still dripping off Jesus, the skies were peeled back, and a voice from heaven called down to earth, saying, "You are my Son, the Beloved; with you I am well pleased" (Luke 3:22). It is significant that Jesus does not receive this designation from heaven until after he has identified with the human condition. The identification was so total and complete that we must hear God saying these same words about us. We too are the beloved of God. That's not because we finally found a way to get our lives cleaned up, but because we belong to God, and in Christ the lost have been found. And that is the only thing that makes human life right.

This is the most critical subtext of all of human life. Until we hear this voice from heaven claiming that we are cherished by a God who is well-pleased with us, we will never be able to truly cherish anyone or believe that we are their beloved as well. We have to receive love in order to give it. And the primal love has to come from the God whom Jesus called Father.

I am amazed at the number of adults in the congregation I serve who still struggle with their parents. Typically the issue is that no matter how hard they tried, they could never get their moms or dads to say, "I love you and am so pleased with you." But that is exactly what the Father in heaven claims. This is not just a spiritual metaphor of father, but the real Father. The work of the Spirit is to adopt us into the Son's beloved relationship with his Father, making us heirs of God, joint heirs with Jesus Christ (Rom. 8:17). And this Father cherishes all of his children. Until we receive that love, which has come by sheer grace, we will spend the rest of our lives in the futile efforts of making our parents well-pleased. Even parents who were good at affirming their love for their children can only provide a pale approximation of the grace that comes only from heaven. The human soul yearns most of all to be cherished by its Creator-Father.

Not only do we have to receive the love of God in order to give love to others, but we also have to receive it in order to work in freedom. As long as we are working without a conviction that we are already cherished, we will try to manipulate the workplace into our source of self-esteem. This is what Sally McGrath was attempting to do with her volunteerism. Churches are filled with people who try to find their worth by making themselves necessary, when they, like Sally, yearn to be cherished. No one finds self-esteem by being necessary. It comes only through being loved, which can only be offered as a free gift. God loves us not as a necessity but as a choice. Only those who believe this are free to allow work to be just work and not their savior, and there is no other way to enjoy working.

This gracious love of God is also the core issue that the pastor is dealing with when speaking to people who are filled with fear. In all of my years of pastoral care, I have never talked anyone out of being afraid, although I've certainly tried. No one is argued out of fear. We can only be loved out of it. And according to the Bible, that is exactly what the perfect love of God does: It casts out fear (1 John 4:18). This is why Jesus, who was so forgiving of his followers' doubts, was so relentlessly harsh on their fears. Those who were afraid to leave home, the servant who buried his talent in a hole out of fear of losing it, the panicked disciples caught in a storm at sea, Peter's terror over failing to walk on water — all were met with the most stern rebukes. "Fear not" is one of Jesus' most frequently repeated phrases. This is because the enemy of our faith is not doubt but fear. Our level of fear is the indication of how little of God's perfect love we've received. No one gets caught up in God's drama for their lives without having to take huge risks, and nothing can interrupt the drama like being afraid to take those risks. Those who believe they are the beloved move from one risk to the next, not because they expect to always succeed, but because they don't care if they fail. How bad can the failure be? They can't lose the love of God.

Since this subtext of being the beloved of God lies beneath so many presenting issues, minor poets can never run out of love sonnets. We have to keep finding new ways of saying the same thing: "You are the beloved of God." But it is important that we not become sentimental about this love. The Scriptures make it clear that God chastens and disciplines those who are loved (Rev. 3:19). This is no ordinary lover we have; this one will be impossible to manipulate. It is God who molds us, and sometimes that hurts. Love isn't always easy on us, but it is always our salvation.

Humans are forgiven.

Grace means that we receive what we need, not what we deserve. That makes it a prophetic doctrine to contemporary society, which is preoccupied with insuring that we all get just what we deserve. Anything less, we claim, is a violation of our rights. But when it comes to God, the last thing we want is what we deserve by rights. What we really want is what we need, and that's to be forgiven.

Many of those who stand in church and gently smile as they sing "Amazing Grace" are familiar with the claim that even "a wretch like me" is forgiven, although most of us are not really convinced about the wretch part. That means that the hymn is probably too familiar to still speak with its original power. Sin is anything that separates us from God and makes it impossible to believe that we are the beloved of anybody. Nothing could be more wretched. Few of us would claim that we are not sinners, and certainly none of those who come to church to sing about amazing grace. We just don't think our sins are all that impressive. But the effect of all sin, especially the sin of thinking that we are not very big sinners, is to leave us alienated from God and thus from others and even ourselves.

The only path home from this alienation is through confession and acceptance of the forgiveness that Jesus Christ was quite literally dying to give us.

When the pastor is speaking on this core doctrine of the church, it is important for him or her to follow the flow of the major poetry in our tradition. For example, John Calvin claimed that we do not tell people to confess and repent of their sins in order to be forgiven. We tell them that they are forgiven so that they can now repent and make changes in their lives.[2] In the New Testament, to be forgiven means to be free, and there is no way to be free to tell the truth or to turn from the things that pull us from God without the hope of forgiveness. So the minor poet doesn't stand in the pulpit to scold the congregation by essentially calling them bad dogs. It is striking how much of contemporary preaching reduces to this: "You bad, bad dogs! Look at what you did." And those in the pews respectfully cower and look like guilty golden retrievers who know they have disappointed the master once again. But the question isn't really "Are we bad?" The question is "What can be done about it?" That is why the preacher begins with the good news of forgiving grace. Only then can we expose ourselves to the depths of our sin and what it has cost God and us. And only then can we accept the invitation to come back home where we belong.

The Gospel-writer Mark tells us that when Jesus was at home in Capernaum, a crowd filled the house to hear his words. Four men who

2. John Calvin, *Institutes of the Christian Religion*, 2 vols., ed. John T. McNeill, trans. Ford Lewis Battles (Philadelphia: Westminster Press, 1960), 3.4.

were determined to get their paralyzed friend in front of Jesus ripped a hole in the roof of the house to lower him down. When Jesus saw their faith — the tradition of belief that precedes a change in an individual's life — he said to the man, "Son, your sins are forgiven" (Mark 2:5). This created quite a stir among the scribes, who wondered, as we do, why Jesus began this healing ministry by forgiving the man's sins. On other occasions Jesus himself made it clear that not all sickness is caused by sin (John 9:1-5). But here, in front of this crowd at his home, Jesus wanted to make the point that he has the authority to forgive sins. After making this claim, he then told the man to stand up, take his mat, and go to his home. The amazing grace stunned the crowd, who said, "We have never seen anything like this" (Mark 2:12).

This is an important text to the minor poet, who finds within it the incredible insight that nothing cripples us like shame. And we will never be able to walk home to ourselves unless we are first at home with Jesus, the only one who can wash away our guilt. The pastor is constantly confronting those whose pilgrimage through life has been interrupted by what they have done and what they have left undone, and the guilt makes it impossible for them to move ahead in life with freedom. It doesn't help for them to attempt to manage the shame by trying to find a way to atone for their sin themselves. Nor does it help for them to ignore the shame, wallow in it, or explain it away. All of that only leads to more guilt. The only hope for any of us is to allow the tradition of faith to carry us to Jesus. Then, when we have heard the declaration of forgiveness, the time comes for us to stand up and walk away from the shame.

Humans are called.

The Bible never pulls apart conversion and vocation. But we often do. We tend to worry most of all about people becoming Christian, and then after they have had a conversion experience, we eventually get around to helping them discern their calling in life. By contrast, all of the stories of conversion in the Scriptures are also stories of calling. When a life is changed by the grace of God, it is for a purpose — to participate in God's ongoing mission in the world. Abraham was blessed to be a blessing. Moses was taken out of the waters as a baby to grow up and lead the people through the waters of the Red Sea. David was converted from a shepherd to a king with a heart for the flock of God. Saul the persecutor of the church became Paul the apostle in a solitary moment when the Lord announced, "He is an instrument whom I have chosen to bring my name before Gentiles and kings and before the people of Israel . . ." (Acts 9:15). That's the way the major poetry explains God's call in all of our lives. It's impossible to keep explaining to people that they have been blessed by grace without also helping them to see how they can be a blessing, which is also a grace.

Whenever someone makes an appointment to talk to me about "calling," I know that we're probably going to be talking about resumes. It is a particularly American preoccupation to reduce God's call to job descriptions. The Apostle Paul's actual job description was to be a tentmaker, but his calling was to bring the name of the Lord before everyone he met, whether it was a king or just someone interested in buying a tent. I have a strong hunch that God is not nearly as worried about how we earn an income as what we do with the name of the Lord along the way. In other words, the real issue is this: Are we being the blessing of God to those around us?

To bless people literally means to give them the bliss of heaven. Nothing does that better than connecting heaven and earth in the name of Jesus Christ. Our calling, then, is less about what we do than it is about who we are — those who reveal the name of the Lord by being what C. S. Lewis called "a little Christ" to others.[3] Of course, that is possible only if the blesser lives in Christ.

Calling begins with identity, not task. The doing has to flow out of the being, because if we aren't clear about who we are, we'll never know what to do with our lives. Again, our culture sees this exactly the opposite way. It assumes that we can change who we are by changing what we do. If you're not happy with life, according to this contemporary mythology, you just have to do something else, or do it with someone else, or do it someplace else, and your whole being will improve. But that never works out for us. Identity is not improved upon by what we do. If we're not happy with life, according to the Bible, we have to take it up with the Creator of that life. Only then do we become renewed in our identity as cherished children of this God. This may still not give us happiness, but it does give us God, and at that point we are much less concerned about finding such fleeting emotions as happiness. That is what the major poetry of our Scriptures really means by conversion. It profoundly transforms us from a people who were

3. C. S. Lewis, *Mere Christianity* (New York: HarperCollins Publishers, 1980), p. 177.

once enslaved to the illusion that we can re-create our lives by what we do, to a people who have come to rest in the blessing of being adopted sons and daughters of God. Only then are we finally able to be God's blessing in the world around us, which is the calling of the conversion.

Anyone can describe doing. Our society is not short on people who are experts on how to get more done, more efficiently and more successfully. But it takes a poet to describe being. That is why people have pastors.

Even a minor poet knows that a calling isn't always fulfilling, which is yet another contemporary lien that we've placed on the biblical truth of having a mission in life. When people criticize their present work by lamenting, "It just isn't fulfilling," what they usually mean is that it doesn't make them very happy. And when they bring this complaint to the pastor, what they're often looking for is support to get a different job. I usually shrug my shoulders and tell them to go ahead and change their workplace if they want to, but not to expect that to make them fulfilled. If they haven't left my study at that point, I continue to tell them that this is the wrong search. The better search is for communion with God. As they rest in that primary mission, they will soon know what to do even if it isn't in a place they had dreamed of spending their lives. Callings, like the rest of life, are not achieved but received.

Any survey of the biographies of the men and women of the Bible who were caught up in this drama reveals that God is not easy on those who are called. At the end of their lives, the best of them were beaten up and taped together. It almost seems that they had been overused in the biblical story. But all of them seemed content. That's because their joy came from being God's blessing along the way.

An Illustration of Calling

Jack and Betty had sold their big house on the hill several years before I arrived as their new pastor. It was the house where they had raised three children and collected over thirty years of cherished memories. It was their home. They were now living in a two-bedroom apartment in another part of town.[4]

---

4. A version of this story first appeared as "Pastoring, at Times with Words," in *Leadership* 26, no. 2 (Spring 2005), p. 106.

It looked to me like Jack was always bothered by something. Betty seemed delightful but a bit spacey. Often as they were leaving church, she would say something odd, but her countenance was so bright that I just smiled and enjoyed her joy. They were always together: one scowling, the other oblivious, but always together.

One day they stopped at the door where I was standing after worship to invite me to their place for dinner. I glibly told them that I would be happy to come if we could find a good time. That's pastor-code talk for "I'm really too busy right now." But Jack wasn't buying it. When I received his third invitation, my secretary (usually the wisest person on a church staff) convinced me to schedule a time to have dinner with them. "After all," she said, "you're the pastor." The call was really that simple.

Once I arrived at their apartment on the appointed evening, it didn't take me long to realize that Betty had Alzheimer's disease. It now seemed so obvious that I felt foolish for missing it earlier. Jack never let her out of his sight. It was then that I realized that he hadn't been scowling for the last couple of years. He was just worried.

Before I even had my coat off, Betty took me by the hand and led me to the painting above the sofa that depicted their stately old home. She became a bit more lucid as the stories of the old place tumbled out of her soul. I felt her squeeze my hand as she talked, reminding me of her subtext: "There is more to me than you see now." Jack stood behind us and allowed his worry to ease a bit with a tender smile. We then made our way down the gallery of photographs in the hallway, where so many memories of better days were hanging on the wall. As she walked up and down that hall, day after day, the old pictures must have whispered to Betty, "Please don't forget us."

Dinner was interesting. Betty couldn't be allowed near the stove, and Jack wasn't about to learn to cook. So he had asked their housekeeper to make them an extra-large omelet before she left that afternoon. When we were ready to eat, Jack put the egg dish in the microwave, then cut it into thirds and served it on Betty's best china. For desert he brought out Klondike bars that we ate using the good silverware, which wasn't easy. Several times during the meal, Betty got up and wandered around the apartment a bit. I was impressed by Jack's ability to maintain our conversation, which was always of secondary importance to him, while always watching his wife.

Throughout the evening I kept thinking that I needed to say something useful. *After all, I'm the pastor,* I reminded myself. But how profound could I be with Betty, whose mind was too clouded for conversation? What would I even say to Jack about this difficult calling? I could try "Keep up the good work" or "This must be really hard," but that would be so inane.

After dinner, we left the old dining-room table and made our way back to the living room sofa, where I sat next to Betty. Jack took the chair across from us. I began to talk, trying to speak of deeper things, but I wasn't doing well. I knew that I was called there to be a blessing to them and wanted desperately to witness to Christ's presence among them. But how? I felt like a pilot circling above the clouds, looking for an opening to land. Soon Betty got up and wandered off again.

When she returned, she stood behind the chair where Jack was seated and put her trembling hand on his shoulder. As only old lovers know how to do, he reached up to take her hand as if it were the first and millionth time he had done it. I stopped talking as they both smiled at me.

Well, there it was — the blessed presence of Christ. Then I knew that I wasn't there to say a thing. My calling was to behold and be amazed. It was as if their mutual smile said, "Don't you dare pity us. We are blessed." Beneath the gentle act of holding a trembling hand lies the mystery of a real marriage that binds two together as tightly as Christ is bound to his beloved church. For better or worse, for richer or poorer, in sickness and in health.

In the end, this is as good as the calling to love can be. There is neither glib sentimentality nor despair. There is just the holding of hands, and perhaps the smile of even God. And I got to witness this holy, intimate moment. After all, I'm the pastor.

CHAPTER 8

The Subtext of the Poet

That night, as I finally drove home from the hospital, a gentle, cleansing rain began to fall. Ahead of me were only the blurred taillights of people for whom I had no responsibility. The hypnotic rhythm of the windshield wipers beckoned me into the refuge of my own world, where I could finally surrender to the fatigue that was all mine.

When I pulled into my driveway, I assumed I would head upstairs to bed, but once inside I realized I was too far gone for that. Too tired to sleep and too restless to talk coherently to my wife, I opted for a cup of tea and my first glance at the morning paper she had saved for me on the kitchen table. But I had neither the ability nor the interest to take in more pathos. So I shoved the paper aside, leaned back in the chair, and stared into the wisps of steam that reached up out of my teacup.

All of the conversations of the day began to reappear — the staff appointments and committee meetings, the phone calls, Carol and Bob Stratton, the church dinner, Sally McGrath, and most of all, that visit with Mr. Jefferson. Then the words from my morning sermon preparation slipped back in: "Enter through the narrow gate . . ."

MINOR POETS HAVE TO STRUGGLE for their poetry. It comes only as a prize bestowed upon those with the courage to keep returning to the wrestling turmoil between the holy words of the Bible and the day's ordinary words. At the end of the day, it's up to the parish poet to make holy sense of all these words.

This is what pastors really mean when they complain about the loneliness of their calling. No one can do this priestly work for them, or even with them. It is ironic that a profession that surrounds pastors with so many people leaves them alone with their own ponderings. And this is the part of the profession that is completely missed by everyone the pastor serves. The members of the church envy their pastor for the many relationships that seem to come as perks of the job. They aren't there to see what happens after all the meetings and visits are done, when the pastor is forced to make the solitary journey into the Holy of Holies to offer exhausted prayers over a cup of tea.

There is nothing hierarchical or elitist about this loneliest dimension of the job. To the contrary, pastors are never more servants of the church than when they're alone with their thoughts about what God is doing in the lives of others. But they're not really alone. Their souls are crowded with all who have made their way deep inside. And of course, there is also the nagging presence of those holy words that will not go away. This is how pastors love their congregations — they take them into their souls, where they carry on both sides of a conversation between the people and their God.

The Poet's Negative Capability

Since their souls are a sacred meeting ground, it is critical that pastors know how to expose themselves to God. It is not enough that they have learned as minor poets how to peer into the subtexts of the Bible and the congregation. They also have to attend to the underlying holy space of their own lives.

It's not the most important subtext, and pastors have to constantly guard against making their personal issues *the issue* for the congregation. Nothing is more dangerous to a church than for its pastor to manipulate it into a means of working out his or her own anxieties, hurts, anger, or unfulfilled yearnings. That reduces the priestly arena into a therapeutic couch for the pastor. This is not to say that pastors cannot have these issues, but when they appear, it is best for them to make use of their own referral list to receive the assistance of trained therapists. Not everything about the pastor belongs to the congregation, and that would certainly include the wounds that the pastor has collected along the way in life.[1] Challenging the notion that poets have only to look within themselves to find their message, T. S. Eliot has claimed, ". . . the poet has not a personality to express, but a particular medium, which is only a medium and not a personality, in which impressions and experiences combine in peculiar and unexpected ways."[2] The pastor maintains a conversation not between the congregation and the pastor but between the people and the God in whose image they are made. Often this holy discourse cannot occur unless the pastor brackets out the personal issues that keep interrupting it.

While mindful of this caution, it is still critical that the minor poet knows how to stand before God with an open soul. That's the place where sermons, counseling, and the best leadership of the church finally occur. After the ears, the eyes, and even the mind are done, and there are no more appointments left in the day, a pastor has to retreat into the soul to wait for holy words.

Minor poets train their souls for their high calling by constantly moving beyond the rationalistic means of handling Scripture and congregations. They don't ignore these necessary exegetical and analytical tools, which provide a critical introduction to the text of the Bible and the organizations they serve, but as poets they know that when all that work is done, they still have miles to go before they sleep. This is what distinguishes the pastor from the scholar. Only pastors have the calling of plunging beneath these texts into their own souls, where they must struggle over the enigma of subtext. And that means that pastors have to become familiar — though never comfortable — with mystery.

The major poet John Keats introduced the importance of negative capability for the writing of poetry: "Negative capability is when man is capable of being in uncertainties, mysteries, and doubt without any irritable reaching after fact and reason."[3] Day after day the parish poet encounters

---

1. One of the frequent conversations I have with my colleagues on the seminary faculty is how do we best respond to those students who have begun the ordination process as a means of finding healing from their hurts. We worry about this because the flock doesn't serve the shepherd; it is the shepherd who serves the flock. Often, when a pastor burns out within five years of being ordained, it is because there was confusion about this fundamental order of service.

2. T. S. Eliot, "Tradition and the Individual Talent," in *The Sacred Wood: Essays on Poetry and Criticism* (London: Methuen & Co., Ltd., 1920), p. 56.

3. *John Keats: Selected Letters,* ed. Robert Gittings (New York: Oxford University Press, 2002), p. 41.

that which does not make sense. Why do children die? Why do the evil prosper? Why doesn't a powerful God prevent pancreatic cancer in the life of a righteous man like Mr. Jefferson? Why? Why? Why? The question will not go away. Every effort to paste easy answers over these pressing questions is only more "irritable reaching after fact and reason." But the questions still must be asked. Like Job, the pastor stands before the whirlwind and dares to contend with the Almighty. Not because answers are expected, but simply because this is the poetic calling. Poets bear the confusion of their people in their own souls, which means that they don't just know the congregation's questions but feel the theological angst they create. And they understand to whom this confusion must be addressed even if they also realize that no rational explanation will be provided.

Like Job, the poet also expects that in time a response will come. This response will not make sense of the pathos of the congregation, but it will make such explanations unnecessary, as Job 38 makes clear: "Then the LORD answered Job out of the whirlwind: 'Who is this that darkens counsel by words without knowledge? . . . Where were you when I laid the foundation of the earth? Tell me, if you have understanding'" (vv. 1-2, 4). The next four chapters continue to accent the mysteries of the Creator to the limited mind of the creatures. And at the end of this terrifying encounter with God, all that Job can say is, "I have uttered what I did not understand, things too wonderful for me, which I did not know" (Job 42:3). It is significant that this affirmation of faith occurred before any of God's blessings to Job's life were restored. Job is grateful not for what God does, but for who God is. That's the purpose of all worship, which frees us to become lost in the beauty of a God we get to behold. And that is what the minor poet is constantly experiencing. Again, in the words of Keats, "With a great poet the sense of beauty overcomes every other consideration, or rather obliterates all consideration."[4] Understanding beauty is really beside the point.

In *The Divine Comedy*, Dante's great pilgrimage through hell, purgatory, and paradise also ends not in explanations but in worship before the incredible beauty, where all of his questions evaporate. "And I who was approaching now the end of all man's yearning, strained with all of the force in me to raise my burning longing high. . . . The beauty I saw there goes far beyond all mortal reach: I think that only He who made it knows the full

4. Keats, *Selected Letters*, p. 42.

joy of its being."[5] This yearning to behold is a call to worship before the beauty of a God to whom we belong. At that point in the journey, all need for rationalisms is lost. No one can make this pilgrimage without being led by a poet.

The journey from confusion to beholding beauty is strange to the members of the church who live in a society that still functions on the assumptions of the Enlightenment. They assume that if they can understand a problem, they can find its solutions. That's why they need a parish poet who knows how to lead them through to the conclusion of their struggle that ends not in solutions but in worship. Since true worship is conducted only in spirit and truth, it can only unfold when their poet is adept with his or her own soul (John 4:23). Pastors lead from the inside out.

Finding the Poetic Voices

After minor poets become accustomed to delving into their souls to find their poetry, they still have to discern how to find their way out of mysterious confusion and into beatific visions. T. S. Eliot has provided a helpful map for this journey in an essay titled "The Three Voices of Poetry."[6] His intent was to provide assistance to poets by unfolding the necessary development in their thinking. Each of the three voices has its own integrity, each belongs to the poet, and it is possible to remain in any one of them, but it is important to know at any given time in which voice one is writing. Although Eliot wasn't writing for the parish clergy, his insights provide great help to all who are trying to emerge out of their brooding over ordinary and holy words with something to say.

The First Voice

Initially the poet isn't focused on saying a thing. When working in the first voice, all of the attention is directed to a burden that weighs heavy in the

5. Dante, *The Divine Comedy*, vol. 3: *Paradiso*, trans. Mark Musa (London: Penguin Books, 1984), XXXIII, XXX, pp. 391, 353.

6. T. S. Eliot, "The Three Voices of Poetry," in *On Poetry and Poets* (New York: Farrar, Straus & Cudahy, 1957), p. 96.

poet's soul, so heavy that the only devotion is to finding relief. This is just as true when the burden is overwhelming gratitude as when it's a screeching lament. Whatever it is, it will not be ignored. Eliot claims that in this stage the poet "is haunted by a demon, a demon against which he feels powerless, because in its first manifestation it has no face, no name, nothing; and the words, the poem he makes, are a kind of exorcism of this demon."[7] Eliot's metaphor may not be preferable to pastor-poets, but we do get his point about being possessed by something we cannot even describe. That something may be the pathos of the parishioner who is caught between how it is and how it ought to be. It may be the our inability to stop crying while baptizing a smiling baby with Down syndrome. Or it may simply be the day's collection of stories.

At this point, poets are only talking to themselves, and even that is saying too much. They ponder experiences they cannot adequately describe. "What was that about?" they ask over and over. Whether they realize it or not, parish poets are asking this question of Jesus Christ, the only one who can exorcise this thing that has possessed them. This is why they have to ask their questions out of their souls and not just their minds. Pastors don't think of their parishioners' experiences as puzzles to be figured out, but as spiritual struggles to discover the God who is in this thing that has now taken over their souls as well their parishioners.

This is not to say that pastors feel their parishioners' feelings. Parish poets don't have the burden of feeling lonely after talking with a widower who misses his wife any more than they should feel sick after visiting someone in the hospital or act as if it's their party when attending someone's birthday celebration. It isn't empathy that possesses the poet — empathy in the sense of feeling what others feel. The poet is possessed by a burden to ask what God is up to in the lives of the lonely and the sick, as well as in the lives of those whose blessings are so abundant that they cannot even count them. The clergy has made a great mistake in accepting the therapeutic language of empathy as a means of fulfilling their callings. Technically, to be empathetic means to project oneself into another person in order to identify with their feelings. And technically that is quite impossible. It is significant that the word *empathy* didn't even appear in the Oxford English Dictionary until 1931, and it wasn't adopted into popular language until after the Second World War.[8] It is a

7. Eliot, "The Three Voices of Poetry," p. 107.
8. For the citation on these dates, and a more thorough critique of the use of empathy

twentieth-century invention that achieved popularity about the same time that we were beginning to make all things center on the self. Now we think that even the feelings of others can be absorbed by us as well. No responsible poet who cherishes the privacy of the soul as a place to encounter God would make such a claim. And no parish poet would dilute his or her calling to such horizontal relationships after taking vows to discover what God is doing with these feelings that are being so intensely felt by parishioners.

For the pastor, the relevant biblical concept is not empathy but compassion, which means to suffer alongside. It is enough of a burden to have compassion for those whose lives have been interrupted, for better or for worse, and to struggle for a line of poetry that will reveal more of the Savior's compassion. As I sat at my kitchen table that night and pondered the great disconnect between the biblical call to enter through the narrow gate and all of the burdens my parishioners were carrying through life, I wondered how they could possibly drop them in order to fit through that gate. And that dilemma was my own burden as their poet.

Returning to Eliot, we are cautioned that "the most bungling form of obscurity is that of the poet who has not been able to express himself *to* himself; the shoddiest form is found when the poet is trying to persuade himself that he has something to say when he hasn't."[9] Until the pastor has struggled to find a compassionate Word for that which remains wordless, there really is nothing to say. Sometimes this struggle occurs in the pastor's study while he is working on the Sunday sermon, and sometimes it occurs while he is staring into a cup of tea at the end of a long day. Always it occurs in the pastor's soul.

No element of the minor poet's job description is more crucial than this churning. The experiences, impressions, befuddlements, and penetrating words that are absorbed throughout the day have to turn over and over in the pastor's soul, where they're mixed together with the holy words of the Scriptures until at last the human subtext can be described with minor poetry. A similar image is provided by Henry David Thoreau: "Know your own bone: gnaw at it, bury it, unearth it, and gnaw at it still."[10] There is no formula for knowing when the churning and gnawing are done. It

by the clergy, see Edwin H. Friedman, *A Failure of Nerve: Leadership in the Age of the Quick Fix* (Bethesda, Md.: The Edwin Friedman Estate/Trust, 1999), p. 179.

9. Eliot, "The Three Voices of Poetry," p. 108.

10. Thoreau, quoted by Annie Dillard, *The Writing Life* (New York: Harper Perennial, 1990), p. 68.

isn't over until it can be expressed, but the preacher prays it will not last longer than Saturday night.

The Second Voice

While the first voice is about finding, the second is about describing. Something was discovered in the marrow of all that gnawing that is so thrilling to the poet that it has to be expressed. This is as much for the joy of the poet as it is for the benefit of those who will receive the carefully woven words that describe the discovery. While this second voice is used in pastoral counseling, on retreats, and in the various expression of parish leadership, it is most evident in the high drama of writing sermons.

Midway through the week, I am never as certain of my destination with the sermon as I was when I planned the preaching schedule. I stay with the same text. I work with outlines and try to keep focused on the point. I've even tried taping the main idea of the sermon to the top of my computer screen. But it always ends up as a different message than I had intended to write. Often it feels like the sermon has taken a distracting detour, and I struggle to get it back on track. Eventually I discover it changed course to head to a new place. One of the most courageous things preachers have to do is relinquish control over the destination and pray that the altered course is a holy intervention.

Poetry has to work itself out of the poet. If I needed formulas and predictable results, I picked the wrong profession. Like the Hebrews in the Sinai desert, a preacher has to watch deliverance unfold along the way. When I am trudging through the work, lost in the desert, I know that a sacred surprise could interrupt at any moment. I live by my faith in those surprises. It's the manna that just keeps showing up, never more than I need, and never late, but after all these years still a surprise.

The Gospels constantly confront us with the startling grace of Jesus Christ. John the Baptist thought the Messiah would bring fire and judgment, but surprisingly he brought forgiveness and redemption. The disciples thought their Lord was going to bring about a kingdom of earthly power, but they were amazed to discover his vision was for the Kingdom of God. Mary and Martha thought their beloved friend would prevent the death of Lazarus, but they were stunned to discover that he was the resurrection and the life. Everyone thought the cross was the end of the story, and that is why preachers always present Easter as startling surprise.

Nothing has changed. Every preacher must begin the week with the reminder that there is more to Jesus than we know. As we hover over the texts and dive into mysterious subtexts, both biblical and human, parish poets are humbled by the discovery of a Jesus who is constantly interrupting our expectations. The purpose of these sacred interruptions is not to impart clever new insights, but to reveal the unapparent holiness. That is what the preacher gets to do when Sunday finally rolls around — reveal the God who is with us.

No one in the sanctuary should be more excited about the Sunday sermon than the person in the pulpit. It is as if the preacher has returned from a difficult and relentless adventure to find a buried treasure, and now the time has come to unveil the discovery. If the preacher isn't thrilled by the sermon, why should anyone in the pews care about it? Everyone loves to watch those who enjoy their work, whether it's Zubin Meta enraptured as he conducts a symphony without a note in front of him, or Rosie at the diner who knows just how to pour a cup of coffee and with whom to flirt and tease. The unspoken secret to great preaching is that no one should enjoy the sermon more than the preacher. This is not because he or she is so impressed with the eloquence of the chosen words. Sermons with too much ornamentation are distracting and even irritating to the congregation. The contagious excitement of preachers, the thing that keeps them awake Saturday night with all of the anticipation of a child on the night before Christmas, is that they cannot wait for the gift of getting to proclaim what they have discovered. This is why the Gospel is called good news.

Sometimes the goodness of the Gospel is expressed with exuberance over our cups that overflow with gratitude for the blessings from God. At other times it is expressed with prophetic warning. Being cautioned that our lifestyles are eating away at our souls is also good news if the sermon presents another way to live. And then there are times when the preacher invites the congregation to enter the same ponderous journey that their poet has taken in recent days.

Many years ago I heard a profound sermon I'll never forget that illustrates this "journey with me" voice of a preacher. It was delivered by an older pastor who was grappling with a text on the rapture from the fourth chapter of First Thessalonians. He began with this startling claim: "This

115

text is an embarrassment." This made the congregation sit up in their pews, afraid they were about to hear heresy. The preacher explained how his own theological commitments made it hard for him to believe in the popular "Left Behind" literature that used this text for its biblical support. He then moved along to explain the function of this epistle to its first readers, who were yearning for the return of the Lord and desperately needed a word of hope. After that, he explained how much we all need the hope of a coming Savior, regardless of our thoughts about particular schemes for his return. Without this hope, he claimed, we live as if we are on our own, which only leads to more despair. And this despair is at the root of most of our favorite sins. Finally, at the conclusion of the sermon, the old preacher returned to his opening lines by saying, "This text is an embarrassment — because we do not have the hope of the early church." As he unfolded this sermon, everyone in the sanctuary could see him sitting in his study the previous week, wondering why he chose to speak on this text, holding together an unwanted conversation between it and the despair he was encountering in the parish and perhaps in his own life, and then the breakthrough coming when he realized that the real embarrassment was not with the text but with our own hopelessness. Sheer poetry.

Since the preparation of the sermon always begins as a pastoral dilemma to discover what God is doing within the congregation, parish poets don't need to worry about how the message will connect. When speaking in the second voice, poets aren't presenting a few cherished ideas they hope their listeners will find relevant. They are articulating a conversation they have been conducting all week between the people and the Savior, who is often hard to find. The preacher has heard both sides of this sacred conversation, and has taken care to include those voices who didn't make an appointment to see the pastor but whose laments and joys are known because their minor poet has learned to watch them closely as they conduct their ordinary routines. The sermon now belongs not to the preacher, to the congregation, or even to God, but to the holy relationship between all three.

The Third Voice

There are times when a poet creates a dramatic character who says things that cannot originate from the poet. For example, King Richard's famous cry "My kingdom for a horse!" depicts not Shakespeare's own desperation, but his insight into how far the powerful can fall. He needs the king if he wants to express this truth in an incarnate voice, as opposed to the more didactic second voice. Most poets strive for proficiency in using this third voice on occasion, while novelists and playwrights use it exclusively.

Once these characters are created, they have their own personalities that will resist the poet's efforts at making them say something they wouldn't. They aren't mouthpieces. When major poets are writing in this third voice, they have to honor the peculiarities of their creations, who take on their own lives even as their stories are being written. Like all creators, the poet has to give freedom to his or her creatures and then permit them to struggle with their stewardship of it. For this reason, the most poetic characters always reveal complexity and ambiguity. A good poet, according to T. S. Eliot, depicts people who have "an admixture of weakness with either heroic virtue or satanic villainy."[11] This is what gives the characters dimension, making them interesting and accessible to readers. The major poets' success in creating these mixed personalities is the primary reason we regard them as major.

As a minor poet, the pastor has a similar commitment to honor the unique voices of the characters of the Bible. They are not mere illustrations for the point the preacher has already decided to make; they're illustrations of their own point. They cannot be rescued beyond the place where the text leaves them. In the words of Anne Lamott, when dealing with a particular character, we have to "leave him where Jesus flang him."[12] The chances are great that many in the congregation feel left in the same place.

The poetic preacher will insist on more than knowing *about* these biblical personalities and will stay with them until they are known. Most of the people in the pews already know about the biblical characters — when and where they lived, the essential details of their stories, and how their conflicts and troubles were resolved. What they don't know is the soul of these characters, and that is what a minor poet is most interested in discovering for them. Exegesis of the biblical text that tells the stories will only take one so far in this discovery process. To more fully discern what these characters would say to the congregation on any given Sunday, the preacher must live with them all week, invite them in as a third voice in the

11. Eliot, "The Three Voices of Poetry," p. 101.

12. Anne Lamott, *Bird by Bird: Some Instructions on Writing and Life* (New York: Doubleday/Anchor Books, 1995), p. 46.

particular conversation now transpiring between God and the church, and also give them a place in his or her crowded soul.

When writing a sermon on Abraham's attempted sacrifice of Isaac, for instance, it is critical that the preacher maintain the integrity of the patriarch's voice as an ancient Mesopotamian who struggled for faith in the God who made promises to him. He is not a twenty-first-century Christian father. Most of the questions about parenting that we have of this text would be confusing to Abraham, and he has little to say in response to them. But the preacher won't realize that unless the week is spent asking Abraham the parishioners' and the preacher's own soulful questions about fatherhood. "How can a man be expected to sacrifice his son? Today we would put a father in jail for attempting something like this. What are God and Abraham thinking?" Abraham doesn't give us even a hint of wrestling over these pressing questions, and the preacher has to pay attention to his silent reaction to the things that bother us the most about his story. Midway through the week, the preacher decides to treat the text as a metaphor that calls all of us to sacrifice our agendas and dreams for our children. But from the preacher's soul comes the discouraging reminder — made by Abraham, who silently shakes his head — that this was not a metaphor for him. He was really going to kill his son. By the end of the week, the preacher may be the one to become silent, silent enough to allow Abraham to speak about what is of interest to him. Perhaps he will say something like, "I've tried to help God be rational in the past, and it only led to problems. I've finally learned that we're not expected to make sense of God. We're just called to obey." Then the preacher sacrifices all plans to make this sermon about parenting or to rationalize the absurdity of what God called his servant to do. Only then can Abraham's third voice be clearly heard in the holy conversation that has taken a strange turn for which he is most responsible.

After writing sermons for over twenty-five years, I am still amazed at how many times I have to take all of my hard work up the mountain of God, where I lay it out on an altar and prepare to drive a knife through the heart of it. On more than one occasion I have entertained thoughts on a Wednesday or Thursday of just applying to law school in order to be done with the whole business of preaching. And it is usually this third voice that is to blame for my discouragement. Not only do the biblical personalities refuse to be manipulated into what I wanted them to say, but also from the moment they found their way inside of me, they began to ask their own probing questions that I would prefer to ignore. By the end of a week of wrestling with their unwanted interrogation, I find that the hand of the angel has stayed the knife that I was about to thrust into the heart of my calling. And then I hear the voice that blesses me with a message from heaven, the pursuit of which was what got me into the minor poetry business in the first place.

The biblical personalities are a cherished part of the communion of saints. No preacher can find a message from heaven without learning to be silent before them.

Nurturing the Poetic Voices

When the poetry dries up for pastors, they get as lost as their parishioners. It is then that they stop praying and give up expecting much to happen through their preaching or the tender words they offer in pastoral care. No longer believing in their own words, they assume the role of ecclesiastical managers who simply meet expectations. Some coast through the rest of their ministries without ever mentioning a sonnet for the soul again. Their sermons and prayers are little more than strung-together platitudes, and their pastoral care becomes equally petty. Others find that they can no longer live with themselves as ecclesiastical con artists and slowly self-destruct in front of the congregation. Either way, it is deadly to the church. There is no life without poetry, and there is no parish poet once he or she has lost belief in the Word. Even if the parishioners are possessed by too much despair to believe, they at least need to believe that their poet believes.

Since preachers are always caught up in dramatic struggles during their sermon preparation, they have to prepare their souls for this weekly contest. No one will survive it without proper training. That means that the pastor has to be practiced in the spiritual disciplines that exercise the soul and make it strong enough to handle all of the voices that have crowded their way inside. Nothing is more important to the congregation than the pastor's doing whatever it takes to maintain a vibrant spirituality, or the poetry will die for the congregation. There is no magic formula for finding this healthy soul. The pastor simply has to do the very thing he or she calls the congregation to do — read the biblical text devotionally every day, and pray without ceasing.

One of the greatest temptations of those who work with the biblical text in the preparations of sermons is to believe that this is also devotional reading. Sermon-writing and devotions have different purposes, and they're different conversations comprised of different people. The sermon is written with and for the congregation, who is always as present in the preacher's preparations as the God who speaks through the text to them. Devotions are the intimate whispers just between God and the servant, who only wants to hear "You are my beloved." Of course, all sorts of other things can also emerge in the pastor's devotional life, including a few angry screams at God, but after the catharsis dies down, all anyone really needs is to be renewed in the perfect love that casts out fear. Until convinced of this sacred love again, the preacher is incapable of writing sermons without smuggling in anxiety, which never makes for good poetry.

In addition to reading the biblical text devotionally, minor poets also nurture their souls through studying the other major poetry. Certainly this includes both historic and contemporary theologians. It is always frightening to run across the statistics that depict how few serious theology books are read by pastors. The often-heard excuse is that the clergy are just too frantic to find "ideas that work" to take the time to work their way through the thick writing of systematic theologians. But I wonder if the real hesitancy of many pastors to read theology is that they've lost their thirst to learn. They assume that learning is behind them, that now they are fully trained and the mission is to succeed. But pastors are never fully trained. Only those who realize this truth have something new to say to the relentless return of Sunday mornings.

In order to refine their skills at speaking into the subtext of the congregation, it is critical for pastors also to learn from the craft of literary artists, who construct sentences as carefully as painters apply oil onto canvas. In a society where words are now plentiful and used recklessly to manipulate, spin facts, and peddle things no one really needs, the minor poet is one of the few people in parishioners' lives who still treats the combination of words as if it is the fusion of atoms. Put together carefully, these words can do a world of good, and when they are not handled with care, they'll wreak more havoc in a soul than can ever be repaired. Words are never cheap to the poet, whose economy with them depicts the power of each one. So every minor poet needs to learn this careful ordering of words by scheduling time to read major poets and novelists, as much for the caliber of their writing as for the stories they tell. When Eugene Peterson was a pastor, he made a discipline of writing "FD" into his appointment calendar three days a week.[13] If someone wanted to see him during those times, he could explain that he already had a meeting then. They didn't need to know that it was with Fyodor Dostoyevsky.

The poetic voice is also nurtured through participation in a community of minor poets. No poet can make it alone. At the seminary we often caution our students that pastors need pastors, but of a particular type. They need to sit with others who appreciate the poetic dimensions of their calling and are veterans at exploring subtext, even if this is not the language they use. It isn't a support group that minor poets need as much as a little school in which each student is also the teacher. No denominational body can provide this for its pastors; it has to be self-created by those who are passionate about growing in their skills. But every time I've taken the initiative to start this group, I've found other pastors eager to participate. Such a small community can hold its members accountable to the true calling of minor poetry and protect them from the daily temptations to become nonprofit managers. It will encourage, teach, force down necessary but hard readings, model, and provide some solace from the loneliness of the calling. Best of all, this small circle of pastors offers poetic friendships — a community defined by a common devotion to beholding beauty in words and in the Word that lies just beneath the surface.

13. Eugene Peterson, *Under the Unpredictable Plant: An Exploration in Vocational Holiness* (Grand Rapids: William B. Eerdmans, 1992), p. 49.

CHAPTER 9

Writing the Poetry

When the alarm beside my bed rang early the next morning, I got up, shuffled downstairs, let the dog out, and headed out to the porch armed with coffee and a bowl of Grape Nuts. Before long I could see straight enough to give thanks for the grace of a new day. About then my wife came and sat down on the steps beside me. After a quiet kiss she turned to her tea and the morning newspaper. I love sitting beside her on those steps.

Sometimes we talk, and sometimes we just sit, together.

An hour later I headed toward my favorite place in the entire world — my home study. It's where I go to collect manna. I sat behind the desk, breathed in a second cup of the coffee, and opened the biblical text assigned by the daily lectionary. I prayed my way through it, and wrote a single page of reflections about things I could say only to God. Now I was ready to plunge into the sermon.

As I returned to the same biblical passage I had been working on every morning that week, it wasn't long before the words I had been gathering from the congregation also appeared. There they were, sitting on my desk, right next to the Word of God.

Sometimes they talk, and sometimes they just sit, together.

On days like yesterday, God and the congregation talked so long that I was late getting to my appointments. Then I couldn't stop watching as their words circled, tumbled over each other, and struggled to be understood. Other days it seemed to me that they were so frustrated that they tried to give each other the silent treatment. That was when I worried the most. But even that is a lovers' quarrel, and lovers cannot leave each other alone for long. Soon they continued to echo their joys, laments, and yearnings in my soul. Most of all, their yearning for each other. By the end of the week, I was thinking that this could go on forever, as it always has. But the time was rapidly approaching for a Sabbath perspective, which meant that I could no longer ponder and brood over this conversation.

The time had about come for a poet to speak.

WRITING SERMONS is hard work. The disciplines of doing faithful exegesis, plowing through the commentaries and other research, organizing all the thoughts scribbled across the yellow tablet, focusing on the main idea, developing an outline, abandoning gems of insight to the editing floor, and then actually writing the sermon are all enough to leave the preacher exhausted. But that's not the hard part.

The reason that every honest preacher admits to being ambivalent, at best, about writing sermons is that it is frightening. At least, it's frightening when it's done well. That's the vocational hazard with which all poets are all too well-acquainted.

When the time has come to actually write the sermon, I always begin by fidgeting with my chair. I think about other things I have to get done in the course of the day, fight back the demons that tempt me to call an elder about an upcoming committee meeting, and experiment with fonts on the computer. Sheer fear. And the fear comes not because the work is hard but because it requires that I leave the safety of a private life.

Nothing that I do later in the day — none of the meetings, conflicts into which I wade, or heart-wrenching counseling sessions — will require the vulnerability that has already occurred before I even leave that home study. The rest of the day I keep my hand firmly on the lever that controls the drawbridge to my soul. If a meeting becomes too confrontational or if the pathos of a counseling session is too much, I can pull that lever, and up comes the bridge to protect me. But sermon-writing knows no such protection, and can only be done without defense. If any inspiration is going to occur, it can only descend into a wide-open soul.

On Sunday night, I take my first serious look at the text for next Sunday. It is then that the week's long grinding begins. As I continue through my week of preparations, and continue on the journey with the people through the wilderness, I wonder how I will survive along the way. I wonder what this passage really means. And before long I am wondering if this will be the Sunday the elders call a special meeting to discuss the problems with their preacher's sermons. But somewhere along the way in the journey, a manna-like breakthrough occurs. To paraphrase an unnamed poet, just one line of the poem drops from the sky, but thank God for that one line.[1] I never begin to write the sermon without that line from above. It's the little miracle that wins me over and convinces me that this sermon is exactly what the congregation, and I, most need to hear. It comes by the end of every week, but that doesn't prevent me from fretting that it won't arrive this time. And that's how my own faith is strengthened.

At this point I'm no longer struggling to find Christ in the subtext of my parishioners or to find my parishioners in the subtext of the Bible passage. Now the struggle is how to write a twenty-minute piece of minor poetry that reveals this holy mystery.

What follows are several insights I have discovered after years of sitting down at the end of a week of sacred conversations to write some minor poetry. This is not a crash course in homiletics for the novice, a critique of classical approaches to developing sermons, or a series of tips for better preaching. I assume that the preacher already knows all about exegesis of the text, the context, and the fundamentals of good homiletic technique. And this chapter assumes that the preacher has already followed the arguments for discerning subtext discussed in previous chapters. Here I'm simply describing some characteristics of sermon-writing that are unique to those who approach their calling poetically.

Revealing Rather than Arguing

The purpose of poetry is to reveal the mystery and the miracle that lie beneath the ordinary. It doesn't argue, buttress against doubt, or defend. It explores. Then it unveils what it finds in voices such as awe, wonder, irony, or even anger and lament rather than instruction or debate. Poets are seldom accused of being convincing, but the best ones can transform the way we see life.

As a minor poet, the preacher is devoted to finding Jesus Christ, the

---

1. Annie Dillard, *The Writing Life* (New York: Harper Perennial, 1990), p. 75.

God with us, as the mystery and the miracle beneath everything. The biblical promise is that all things hold together in Jesus Christ (Col. 1:15-20). Pastor-preachers believe in this promise, and they have received the gifts from the Holy Spirit, and the skills from their training, to dig around until they discover just what this Savior is up to in any particular context. It doesn't matter if that context is a particular person, the congregation as a whole, the community around the church, or the pathos of current events. Christ holds all things together. That doesn't leave out much. After a week of excavating the texts of Scripture, the words of the newspaper, and the words expressed in the congregation, the pastor at last discovers this Christ and receives at least a glimpse of how he is holding us together with God.

As a minor poet, on Sunday morning that pastor is less interested in making an argument for the presence of Jesus Christ than in simply showing him to the congregation. Even when preaching out of the New Testament epistles, a poetic preacher doesn't stop at presenting the apostolic arguments, but digs deeper to find the ways in which these truth claims are revealed as the Christ at work in our lives.

It is the difference between knowing about and knowing. While there is a necessary place in the church for learning about this God who is with us, that place is not the pulpit. Preaching, at least the poetic variety, is devoted to knowing God. This is why no congregation can endure for long by offering only worship. It has to offer Sunday school classes for all ages, Bible studies, seminars, and small groups that are all focused on helping their participants know more about God. But in the act of worship on Sunday mornings, the preacher is assisting the congregation in moving deeper into their knowledge of God, which involves a relational experience with God. As Bernard of Clairvaux claimed, all of our cognitive knowledge of God is but a preparation for the subjective encounter with God. Poetic preaching is focused on moving from the cognitive to this subjective encounter.

This is not subjective in the sense of relative, as if it is up to everyone listening to decide what to make of the God the preacher presents. Rather, it simply means that the preacher is focused on subjects of God and the congregation encountering each other. Having introduced this encounter, the preacher can then get out of the way and allow the truth of this holy moment to do the convincing. Nothing is more irritating than having someone interrupt a moment of intimacy, and the last thing the reunited lovers want is a lot of commentary about what this encounter means.

Protestant churches today are filled with people who have learned the right answers to the questions about the content of our faith, but who still yearn for a deeper encounter with the subject of faith. They know the stories of the Bible, the teachings of the prophets and the apostles, and why their particular brand of church has interpreted the Bible the way it has. But in every soul the insatiable thirst for holiness perseveres. The living water that can quench this thirst is not more right information about Jesus. Only Jesus himself will do. And Jesus is not a what; he's a who. So the preacher dare not reduce the person of Christ to orthodox theology about him, or the souls of everyone in church that day will leave as parched as they arrived.

Anyone who has been to Florence to see Michelangelo's *David* knows the qualitatively different experiences of beholding beauty and hearing about it. I had studied Renaissance art at some length, and I assumed I knew a great deal about this masterpiece before I laid eyes on it. But when I finally had the opportunity to stand before it, I wanted never to leave. When preachers think of their sermons less as polemics and more as art, they are allowing the congregation to behold Jesus. Even though few minor poets would want to compare themselves to Renaissance artists, we can still master the craft of creating sermons that beckon those in the pews to behold.

Since minor poetry is devoted to presenting the person of salvation and not simply information about the Savior's work, it is critical that the preacher convey the deeper discovery of Christ that has just been unearthed. It was for this reason that the Holy Spirit led the preacher to the discovery in the days preceding the sermon. While Christ is the same yesterday, today, and forever, there is a particular proclamation of his presence that is germane to this moment in the congregation's pilgrimage. This discovery has no shelf life and has to be used for the purposes the Spirit gave it. When I have tried to gather up the great insights that fell to the editing floor after completing a sermon and store them away in my files, I have later returned and found, to my dismay, their greatness reduced to mediocrity. So these days I use everything I have when I have it, and I throw away the edited material. It is impossible for the discoverer to reveal old discoveries with any sense of wonder. If it is boring to me, it's highly unlikely to spark much enthusiasm in the congregation. And revealing a dull Christ is about the last thing a minor poet cares to do.

Using More Images, Fewer Illustrations

From the time pastors took their first homiletics course in seminary, they have understood the importance of a good illustration or two for their sermons. These illustrations help the thick theology of the sermon appear more relevant and accessible to the congregation. They also invite those in the pews whose thoughts were drifting away during the sermon to come back to the preacher's message. "Everyone loves a good illustration," seminarians are routinely told. That's certainly true. Over the years I have discovered that my congregation remembers my sermon illustrations much better than they do the substantive content of any of my sermons. This is particularly true if the illustration involves a moving story. But I have also discovered that this tempts me to reduce the sermon to the lyrics from a country music song. If the congregation walks away from worship remembering my sad story about a motherless child better than the point about the God who cradles us, then I didn't write the sermon well. My calling is not to move the congregation, but to reveal the extraordinary grace of our Savior, who is the one who moves us into discipleship.

There are two great dangers that accompany every sermon illustration. The first, and most common, is that the illustration will overpower the gentle revelation of Christ that the preacher is trying to hold before those in the pews. The second is that it will be only ornamentation that distracts the listeners from the pristine beauty of the message. This is not to say that preachers should avoid using illustrations. There are times, especially when preaching out of the epistles of the New Testament, when a good illustration is necessary even for the minor poet. But even then, it is important that the illustration not get in the way of the preacher, the congregation, and the Holy Spirit.

The longer I preach, the fewer illustrations I seem to use. Mostly that is because I have learned to trust the incarnational nature of the biblical text. The vast majority of the Bible presents not abstract theology, but theology embodied in sacred stories. These narratives are profoundly compelling, and they don't benefit from being interrupted with similar contemporary stories. The following paragraph illustrates this point:

Our text claims that as Jesus was walking along, he stopped for the blind beggar who interrupted him. This reminds me of something that happened last week as I was driving to the airport to pick up my in-laws from the airport. I was focused on getting there on time, and so I was furious when I had a flat tire. But when the Triple-A man finally arrived, I realized that I shouldn't be a witness of impatience before him. So I tried to take this interruption more seriously and pay attention to this poor man, who was just trying to do his job. He wasn't easy to talk to because he was so rough and just focused on getting his job done, but I knew that I was called to set aside my impatience and treat him as a holy creature. So I asked him about his life . . .

At this point, the congregation is no longer thinking about the interruptability of Jesus and is completely absorbed in the saintly disposition of the preacher. But the preacher cannot save the greasy, slow-moving Triple-A man or anyone in the congregation. What the preacher wanted to say was that Jesus is the God who stops when he hears our cries, and yet the lengthy illustration of this point has led everyone to think that it is their calling to be Jesus. Only Jesus can be Jesus; we are just his witnesses. This is not to say that we should not pay attention to those whom God brings into our path, but that was not the kerygmatic point of either this biblical text or the preacher's sermon.

An alternative illustration from this text could look like the following:

Our text claims that as Jesus was walking along, the blind beggar interrupted him. How often have we all been on the way to something we thought important, only to be interrupted by someone who is in our way? It happened to me just last week, when I was so focused on getting to the airport on time that I was tempted to ignore the man who came along to help me with my flat tire. But Jesus never confuses his mission with getting to a place on time. While I had to stop because of my flat tire, Jesus chooses to stop for the blind beggar because that is what God does.

This second illustration still runs the great risk of distracting listeners for a while, but at least it strives to get back to the point of the text as soon as possible, and that is the agenda of all helpful sermon illustrations. But one has to wonder if even this better illustration is really necessary. The story in the Gospels is already compelling enough to hold the congregation's attention. Ironically, few things can be more subversive to the point of the biblical text than our efforts at illustrating it.

Poets never use illustrations, but they often invoke powerful images. The difference between them is that an illustration is typically an ornament that hangs on the sermon, while an image is always a compelling picture that invites the beholder to look through it into the greater mystery. Illustrations tell stories that exemplify the point of the text. Images embody the point. The Bible has very few illustrations, but it is filled with powerful images. When the first psalm claims that those who delight in the law of the Lord are like trees planted by streams of water, it is providing not an illustration but an image. A preacher can spend the whole sermon on this text, peeling this image like an onion, and never make it to the eternal core.

Ezra Pound wrote, "The image is not an idea. It is a radiant node or cluster, it is what I can, and must perforce, call a vortex, from which and through which and into which ideas are constantly rushing."[2] An image propels ideas into more directions than even the creator of the image could imagine. With this description of imagism, Pound is not far from what the Orthodox Church has long understood as the function of icons. An icon is designed to be not a beautiful work of art, but a window into divine mysteries. It points beyond itself. The design of every authorized icon draws the eyes of those who gaze upon it through the two-dimensional painting into the third and even the fourth dimensions of a subjective encounter with God. That is exactly what the use of images in a sermon can offer. And a minor poet will find them irresistible.

When preaching on a text that contains an image, like the trees planted by streams of water, it is best to stay with it and not introduce competing images. But when preaching on a text that is void of images, the minor poet should feel free to introduce one, and only one, that will invite the listener into the Christ who is waiting in the text. For example, when preaching on justification, the minor poet may invoke the image of a bent ruler that never measures well, like our bent lives. Or a courtroom. Or a broken window. If preaching on the claim in Philippians 1:6 that "the one who began a good work among you will bring it to completion," the preacher may introduce the image of a sculptor who mysteriously chips away at a formless stone, for years, until a life begins to appear. A different sermon on the same text may use the image of a trembling hand in a nursing home to invite the congregation into God's strange ideas about completed goodness.

The power of a great image is found in its deceptive simplicity, which is

2. Ezra Pound, *Gaudier Brezeska: A Memoir* (New York: Lane, 1916), p. 106.

a cherished tool of all poets. Like an illustration, an image can be so powerful that it loses its iconic power and draws attention only to itself. Whenever a preacher has taken too much time to build the image, the chances are great that all of the details will only get in the way of the necessary passage through to the Gospel. It is significant that the Bible doesn't explain its many images, such as vines, shepherds, broken pots, fathers, a narrow gate, and living water. It just invokes them and allows the Holy Spirit to propel readers through the image in diverse ways.

Following a Spiral, Not a Line

Arguments, when presented well, try to prove a thesis. A typical argument in a sermon would be that Christians should love their neighbors. In building the argument for this thesis, a preacher often follows a linear path of logic. An initial clear point is made, such as "Jesus calls us to love our neighbors." Then, after this is established within the biblical text, a second point is made that naturally follows: "We as the disciples of Jesus should do what he tells us." Then maybe a third point is made about why the neighbor needs the love Jesus commands us to give. (Usually this is where a moving illustration is inserted that depicts someone lonely.) Finally, the conclusion of the sermon presents the thesis as convincing, since it is the only logical deduction to draw from this irrefutable line of argument. "So you should love your neighbor." By this point, those in the pews who are still awake will nod their heads in agreement.

Poets don't make arguments; they reveal mysteries. This doesn't mean that minor poets can't state claims in their sermons, but they don't follow a linear path of logic. They don't worry about logic at all. Instead, they explore the sacred mystery that they are attempting to unveil to the congregation. And this typically means that their points follow the path of a spiral. The sermon is not a circle, since it does make progress, but as with all interesting explorations, it doesn't move in a straight line.

The poetic preacher may begin by stating that, of course, we know we ought to love our neighbors, and Jesus is pretty clear about that. But before progressing to an argument for contemporary disciples to obey Jesus, the preacher may spiral back to ask if this commandment is really even possible to obey. How do you make yourself love someone? What was Jesus thinking in asking this impossible thing of us? Now that the congregation has found echoes of their own unexpressed questions of Jesus, the preacher is ready to move ahead by introducing a new point: "No one can love like Jesus." After enjoying this discovery a bit, the preacher spirals back again to engage the new point with both the commandment to love our neighbor and our protests that it is impossible. "Perhaps," the preacher suggests, "the commandment is calling us not to muster up love for the neighbor but to witness how the Christ within us loves even the most unlovable person. Only Jesus can fulfill his commands."[3]

Whenever I approach a familiar text of the Bible, one of my first responsibilities is to get the congregation's assumptions about the text off the table as soon as I can. I don't disprove or discount their familiar perspectives. I just make it clear that this sermon is not going to remind them of what they already know. That initial spiral is the best opportunity to do this, and asking probing questions of the assumptions is the best means. The purpose of this practice is not to be novel or even engaging, but to be faithful to my own assumption as a minor poet that there is more in this major poetry of the Bible than any of us have already discovered.

Another spiral in poetic preaching is the pattern of conversing between the subtext of the biblical text and that of the contemporary context. Most poems have a rhythm, if not a meter, that carries the listener in an eventually familiar pattern through the stanzas. In addition to its own beauty, this rhythm has a function: to reassure the listener when it is not at all clear where one is in the exploration or where it will all end. The minor poet establishes this needed sense of rhythm by consistently moving from the hidden message of the Scriptures to the hidden realities of our own lives. Back and forth, from subtext to subtext, the spirals continually progress in ever-deepening conversation until at last the preacher arrives at the kerygmatic proclamation of the morning. The preacher cannot tarry long in the sermon with either subtext, or the conversation will digress into monologue. Then, as Walter Brueggemann has warned, the sermon will present either an exaggerated sense of the self or an exaggerated sense of God without us.[4] Since the core of our proclamation is that God is indeed with us and we are with God, even when we cannot see that, the preacher

---

3. There are other valid interpretations of this text. My purpose is not to present a hermeneutic of the command to love the neighbor, but to demonstrate the nonlinear path of poetic sermon-writing.

4. Walter Brueggemann, *Finally Comes the Poet: Daring Speech for Proclamation* (Minneapolis: Fortress Press, 1989), p. 50.

has to consciously move back and forth between these two sides of sacred dialogue.

This pattern of spiraling conversation has the added benefit of keeping the congregation engaged in the preacher's message for the same reason anyone stays with an interesting conversation — it is just too riveting to leave. But as a minister of the Word, the preacher does have the burden of bringing the conversation to a concluding and clear proclamation of the Gospel. That conclusion may be more of a whisper, as is the nature of the poet, than a pulpit-pounding declaration, but it stills need to be clear. Penetratingly clear.

It is also helpful to spiral between the grammatical voices that are used in the sermon. At some point in the sermon I try to utilize the first-person voices, both plural and singular, the second-person voices, and occasionally the third-person voices. This variety reflects the way people both think and talk. Every good story, none better than the Gospel, moves easily back and forth between all the voices. The second-person singular, "you," is by far the most powerful and for that reason needs to be used sparingly. I tend to invoke this voice most often in the conclusion to the sermon, where I am trying to leave the message in the souls of those listening to it. The third person, "they," is the safest, but too much of it will distort the sermon into a Gospel that is only for them. Even though in my seminary homiletics courses we were cautioned against this, it is possible to use "I," the first-person singular, but an excessive utilization of this will make the sermon all about me. However, avoiding any use of the first-person singular runs the risk of making the preacher appear to be either a distant professional or a saint who doesn't struggle with these issues that plague the congregation — neither of which is true of a minor poet. And for the preacher to speak only in the first-person plural is to try to hide in the collective "we." So it is best to spiral back and forth between all three voices, plural and singular, in order to say, "The Gospel is for you, them, and certainly me too."

Taking the Time to Explore the Mystery

Poetry refuses to be rushed. Even the shortest poems demand time both in the writing and in the hearing of their discovered mystery. That's because it's the carefully explored nuances that make the mystery glorious. And so the resident minor poet of a congregation has to be disciplined to take the time necessary not only to dig for the mystery of a God with us, but also to write the poetic sermon in such a way as to invite the congregation to slow down. There is a reason why churches don't have drive-through windows. No one grabs the Incarnation on the run.

This makes minor poetry countercultural today. Society strives to make all things, especially our lives, move compulsively faster and faster in order to get more work accomplished, gather more income, assimilate more information, fulfill more obligations at home, and along the way lose more weight. The only thing that we don't seem to have more of is time. So we're always in a hurry. Even as people make their ways into the pews on Sunday mornings, their minds are still racing with the lists of things they have to get accomplished before the weekend is over. "I still have to take care of that loose step on the back porch, get both of the cars washed, and get my spreadsheet put together before work tomorrow morning. Doesn't Tommy have a Little League game this afternoon? And come to think of it, we still have to get a babysitter for him if we're going to that party tonight. I bet I'm not going to make it to the gym today." Suddenly this ever-expanding list is interrupted by the pastor's call to worship. This is why *Sabbath* can be translated from the Hebrew as "Stop," "Cut it out," or "Give it a rest."

Clearly, no one in the pews is yet ready to embark on the preacher's journey in search of the still small voice of God. This is why the sermon is best placed in the worship service after the congregation has spent at least half of the hour slowing down long enough to pay attention to what they're doing in worship. The call to worship, the hymns, the prayers of adoration and confession, and most of all the moments of quiet reflection are designed to open the eyes of the congregation to the deep truth of the sacred encounter in which they are participating. Having stopped to confront the truth that we are sinners who have spent all week rushing past the presence of God, the congregation is at last ready to hear the far deeper truth of God's grace to them. Now the minor poet can climb the steps of their pulpit.

After spending so many hours during the previous week in front of a television, a secular form of Sabbath rest, those in the pews are accustomed to being sold a message in thirty seconds. Then another thirty-second pitch races onto the screen. And another. So even though the body is stretched out on the sofa during all of this, the mind of the viewer is actually moving pretty fast. It's not working hard, but it is moving quickly to the next thing. Essentially the same thing happens when people tire of television and go to their computers to surf the Net. And it's the same thing that happened earlier in the day when they raced through their appointments — they moved quickly without working hard. As a minor poet, the preacher has to invite the congregation to move slower mentally while working harder, the exact opposite of their expertise. Poets are among the last people in society who do not confuse busyness with hard work, and who move slowly to devote themselves to the extraordinarily hard work of paying attention to life.

The Four Gospels never depict Jesus in a hurry. Never. This drives contemporary disciples nuts, since we're hustling all of the time and expect that surely the Savior of the world can keep up with us. But the question of the Gospel is this: Can we move as slowly as Jesus to see what God is doing? That is the burden of minor poetry. This means that a sermon has to challenge the congregation's expectations that its point should be immediately accessible, that it's just one more thing soaring through their lives at breakneck speed, and that if it's not entertaining they should not be blamed for drifting back to working on their lists. That's a significant challenge.

When a preacher responds to the challenge by constructing a Ferrari sermon that can compete with all of the other agendas that are racing through the minds of those in the pews, the contest for their souls is already lost. It doesn't matter how many slick video clips preachers develop to accompany the sermon, or how quickly they speak, or how closely their sermons resemble the routines of stand-up comics, they can never adequately compete with the fast-paced entertainment industry. Even if they could, their congregations would still lose. The prize of hearing the still small voice of God comes not from a race, but from a slow journey that moves carefully in search of what appeared lost.

So as a minor poet, the preacher walks around in the pulpit, looking for the lost coin or the pearl of great value. The sermon turns over all of the furnishings of the congregation's lives in this desperate search. They thought that the newly remodeled kitchen was what they were looking for, but when their preacher looks beneath it, nothing of eternal worth is seen. So the sermon moves on to examine everything else — the job, the vacation, the new car out in the driveway, even the new boyfriend. Still nothing. Along the way in this search, the preacher keeps spiraling back to the text that promises that God does not abandon us. This holy presence is introduced first as a whisper, and then as a firm conviction, and by the end of the sermon as doxology. With eyes to see, we can find the holiness in all things we were turning over and discarding in life because we were just moving too fast to see it.

The pastor lives by the belief that Jesus Christ holds all things together, and it is for this Savior that the harried souls in the pews truly yearn. All their busyness and distracting entertainments were never more than unconscious techniques for coping with that yearning. But the soul belongs to God, and nothing else can cover over its yearning for long. If the congregation didn't believe that, they wouldn't even be in the church. As soon as the congregation has even a glimmer of belief that these really are holy words spilling over from the pulpit, and that they may unveil the presence of the Word made flesh in their lives, they will bring their fast-paced lives to a screeching halt to begin the hard work of listening.

So there they sit, frantic and frazzled, but daring to hope that there really is a sacred Word that can fill their deep yearning. The name of that Word is Jesus Christ, and the minor poet gets to reveal his mysterious presence every Sunday.

Bibliography

Augustine, Bishop of Hippo. *Confessions: Books I-XIII*. Trans. F. J. Shedd. Indianapolis: Hackett Publishing Co., 1993.

Barnes, M. Craig. *Searching for Home: Spirituality for Restless Souls*. Grand Rapids: Brazos Press, 2003.

Bolin, Wilhelm, and Friedrich Jodl. *Ludwig Feuerbach's Sämtliche Werke*. Stuttgart-Bad Cannstalt, 1960.

Brueggemann, Walter. *Finally Comes the Poet: Daring Speech for Proclamation*. Minneapolis: Fortress Press, 1989.

Calvin, John. *Institutes of the Christian Religion*. 2 vols. Ed. John T. McNeill. Trans. Ford Lewis Battles. Philadelphia: Westminster Press, 1960.

Chesterton, G. K. *Orthodoxy*. Colorado Springs: Waterbrook Press, 1994.

Dante. *The Divine Comedy*, vol. 3: *Paradiso*. Trans. Mark Musa. London: Penguin Books, 1984.

Dickinson, Emily. *The Complete Poems of Emily Dickinson*. Boston: Little, Brown, 1960.

Dillard, Annie. *The Writing Life*. New York: Harper Perennial, 1990.

Eliade, Mircea. *The Sacred and the Profane*. New York: Harcourt Brace Jovanovich, 1957.

Eliot, T. S. "The Social Function of Poetry." In *On Poetry and Poets*. Pp. 3-16. New York: Farrar, Straus & Cudahy, 1957.

————. "The Three Voices of Poetry." In *On Poetry and Poets*. Pp. 96-112. New York: Farrar, Straus & Cudahy, 1957.

————. "What Is Minor Poetry?" In *On Poetry and Poets*. Pp. 34-51. New York: Farrar, Straus & Cudahy, 1957.

————. "Tradition and the Individual Talent." In *The Sacred Wood: Essays on Poetry and Criticism*. Pp. 47-59. London: Methuen & Co., Ltd., 1920.

Feuerbach, Ludwig. *Principles of the Philosophy of the Future*. Trans. Manfred Vogel. Indianapolis: Hackett Publishing Co., 1986.

Frankl, Viktor. *Man's Search for Meaning*. New York: Simon & Schuster, 1963.

Friedman, Edwin H. *A Failure of Nerve: Leadership in the Age of the Quick Fix*. Bethesda, Md.: The Edwin Friedman Estate/Trust, 1999.

Gregory the Great. *Pastoral Care*. Ancient Christian Writers: The Works of The Fathers in Translation. Vol. 2. Trans. Henry Davis, S.J. New York: Newman Press, 1950.

Keats, John. *John Keats: Selected Letters*. Ed. Robert Gittings. New York: Oxford University Press, 2002.

Lamott, Anne. *Bird by Bird: Some Instructions on Writing and Life*. New York: Doubleday/Anchor Books, 1995.

Lewis, C. S. *Mere Christianity*. New York: HarperCollins Publishers, 1980.

Lischer, Richard. *Open Secrets: A Memoir of Faith and Discovery*. New York: Broadway Books, 2001.

Nouwen, Henri. *The Genesee Diary: Report from a Trappist Monastery*. Garden City, N.Y.: Image Books, 1976.

Oden, Thomas C. *Pastoral Theology: Essentials of Ministry*. San Francisco: HarperSanFrancisco, 1983.

Otto, Rudolf. *The Idea of the Holy*. London: Oxford University Press, 1923.

Peterson, Eugene. *Under the Unpredictable Plant: An Exploration in Vocational Holiness*. Grand Rapids: William B. Eerdmans, 1992.

Pound, Ezra. *Gaudier Brezeska: A Memoir*. New York: Lane, 1916.

Robinson, Marilynne. *Gilead*. New York: Farrar, Straus & Giroux, 2004.

Schmemann, Alexander. *For the Life of the World*. Crestwood, N.Y.: St. Vladimir's Seminary Press, 2000.

Taylor, Barbara Brown. *Leaving Church: A Memoir of Faith*. San Francisco: HarperSanFrancisco, 2006.

Willimon, William. *Pastor: The Theology and Practice of Ordained Ministry*. Nashville: Abingdon Press, 2002.